AF362477

Going to Buy a Plot
In
Maaĩ Mahiũ

CECILIA GATHONI

Going to Buy a Plot in Maaĩ Mahiũ
©Cecilia Gathoni
ISBN: 9783949651953
First published 2023

An Imprint of independently published book
Edited by Philip Odhiambo
Cover by Erick Muchira

Published by Piefke Trading
www.piefke-trading.com
info@piefke-trading.com

Dedication

To everyone who is happy to live this life the best they can.

Acknowledgements

I would like to thank the following people for their huge efforts towards this book:

Philiph Odhiambo for Proof Reading the manuscript, Melissa Mwita, Grace Kīhoro as beta readers.

I am also thankful to Eric Muchira for the beautiful cover that says everything, and my publisher for guidance in every stage.

I also have special gratitude to my followers on WhatsApp- Your feedback gave these stories to life.

My family for being the butt of most of the jokes. Haha please don't ask me to change my name.

Contents

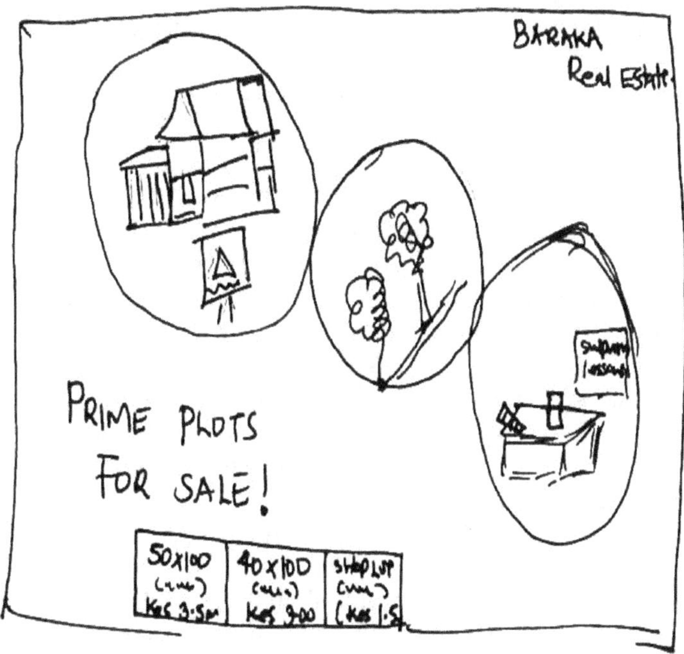

1. Buying A plot in Maaĩ Mahiũ

Part 1

Beef Sausages

It's 7:00 a.m. Monday and you are walking towards Railways to catch a cheaper *mat* to Rongai because these ones here are saying 150/- and if you will come back with another 150 Shillings, living where you live, the total transport expenses in one day including ₉the *boda* fro

m your house will be 660 Shillings. The client will pay you 2000 shillings. Briefly you hear a voice telling you, "*ũyũ ni ũrimũ ũraruta*" but *sasa ukatae kwenda na unga ni mia mbili?*

Of course, *hutakosa kwenda* because you are a woman of middle age who now has to worry about getting a good gynaecologist, a good eye clinic, and a regular visit to a *Muindi* dentist. Before things fall apart.

You are also drinking black seed oil, moringa powder, and *hatha*. And you know these are ordered specially from some Nubian woman in Kibera.

You are also looking into settling down *ata kama ni* Isinya *ni sawa*.

You notice the magazine vendor setting up near Railways and buy one of those noisy leaflets advertising property.

You leaf through it incongruously wondering, *hizi ni watu hununua*?

You decide *enyewe* it's time to do something about your situation because you are going to be 40 without a plot? Even a 50X100 *pale* Ruai?

Sasa hapa ni kujikubali, this is a matter of beginning your self-acceptance journey.

The first thing you do is start to watch Inooro TV so you can know the latest plot offers,

You listen keenly to the commercials that scream at you:

'ŨŨ HIHI NĨŨRENDA KŨGŨRA MŨGŨNDA?

YOU ANSWER, YES! IN YOUR HEART

"No, kaĩ ndirĩ ona ng'e." But *haithuru*, there is nothing wrong with dreaming.

You send a DM to your mother's cousin's wife because you have seen she is into land and plots buying and such.

'Sasa, ni Gathoni,'

You start because being friends on Facebook doesn't mean you know each other.

She is online so she replies right away.

You tell her you would like to buy her lunch and talk about land.

She suggests Wednesday but you have that kid coming in for retouching on Wednesday and it will take a good five hours, so, Wednesday won't do.

"Can we try Thursday?"

She says, 'Come to the office, we can have lunch downstairs,'

You say okay but worry about it a lot because you don't know exactly where she means, it could be one of those places they sell you fried bananas and hard pieces of beef for 600 bob and then you have to drink a KES 250/- 'mixed juice' as you wait for your food to be cooked.

You were hoping it could be one of those places you can check out the menu online and know beforehand how much you can afford to part away with for a meal.

Mko Bomas sasa.

You start to make a mental checklist of your self-acceptance list.

The first thing to do is get a leather jacket.

If you are going to be taken seriously as a prospective land owner, a leather jacket is a crucial wardrobe piece.

You will also need a handbag and brightly colored wedges.

Your mother's cousin's wife has sent you her contact card with a link to available property.

There is a bungalow in Thika six point something Million.

She actually thinks you can buy property.

On Thursday you meet in the office and then go down together to the hotel.

Ah, *kumbe* ni Home lunch.

You admire and despise the establishment in one breath. How do they manage to pull such a crowd and how can you have a conversation here?

But everybody seems to be doing just fine.

You are led to a table between what seems like a car import business meeting going on. Four men with various colours of khaki trousers and mocassins, paired with checked shirts with button pockets, also in different colours from beige, cream, brown, and blue.

On the other side, there are two men, with obviously dyed hair, and a woman in a very shiny dress. Silk? Satin? She also has earrings and a long twist wig. She is holding onto a big Oppo phone and has a toothpick in her mouth, she seems to be directing the meeting.

I can imagine it's a government tender deal on the table. Possibly the one that clinched the Playhouse Highway flowers.

Seasonal flowers in tiny pockets planted vertically. How will the seed fall back into the soil?

"*Si wangeniomba tu* a few succulents?" I have had this thought more than once.
My lunchmate fits in right away. She is in a bright, yellow dress with black dots and yellow wedges.

She has a handbag that could double as a weapon. It has hard sides, with silver spikes all around its surface. She has blonde *muongezo* on her head (Ghanaian). It's very neat but I can hear her hair going 'ting' 'ting' 'ting' all around her scalp.
A month from this she will be back to her hairdresser and she will look at herself in the mirror and sorrowfully ask the shampoo girl.

'*Sasa ni nini inakata* hairline *yangu hivi*?'

The shampoo girl will shrug and tell her, '*Labda ni* scalp *yako iko na shida.*'
Then they will style her hair with a fringe this time to hide the receding hairline.

And before she knows it, her hair will be just bits and pieces so she will either have to shave it all off *ama,* if she spends enough time on IG, she will hear about Sisterlocks and get her problems solved.

The waitress hands us oily menus without making eye contact.

She looks tired and hurried and very very dehydrated. We should go back to compulsory mask-wearing if this is how dry-lipped everybody is and, if this is how freely everyone fishes into their noses in public, *acha tu tuvae* masks.

She orders masala fries with two sausages.
I scan the menu and only feel comfortable with the breakfast things. The arrowroot, and the masala tea.

I ask if the sausages are pork.

She says she will ask.

In the name of health, I ask for *chapati na stew ya minji.*

'Do you want sausages as well?'

The waitress asks.

'Are they pork or beef?'

'They are Farmer's Choice.'

'Ask what they are of then tell me.'

'What will you have as you wait?'

The billion shilling question.

We look over the menu again.

My lunchmate points at the juice. I ask for tea.

'O, you want a mug or a teapot?'

I right away know that's a tea bag affair and ask for a Krest instead. Krest *baridi*.

When she goes, *Wa Kim*, my mother's cousin's wife, whips out her Infinix and shows me a photo of my cousins. This one just graduated from Law School. This one is in the US Army.

I'm looking at a dreadlocked man dressed in camouflage. I have never met him. The lawyer never met him either. *Wa Kim* then swaps to the left and reveals a man dressed as a chief.

'*Mamaguo.*'

'*Haiya, kwani anakuanga chief?*'

'Yes, *alianza kama* headman, now he has been a chief for many years.'

She shows me the car he drives, their house, and their farm in Laikipia where they rear beef cattle.

'I heard you are a writer. You write for Daily Nation?'

She loses interest when I tell her I write online.

She tells me about her trip to Germany.

'*Huko* imagine *hakunanga uchafu*!'

She also tells me that when you are in a plane you can't know it's raining because you are above the clouds. 'It's very nice to ride in a plane.'

Then something clicks in her and jolts her.

'I've heard people make millions from online writing. Can you introduce my son? He is very clever *na ako na kila kitu hadi* WiFi.

She takes my number and sends it to her recently graduated lawyer son.

The food comes, and the waiter has brought two extra sausages, you ask again what they are. She says beef and you say you won't have beef sausages.

She asks, '*Sasa tutafanyaje na* receipt *ishaatoka?*'

You tell her you wanted pork.

She says, 'But there is no pork.'

Wa Kim laughs and says with that typical patronizing tone that characterizes new money, 'Ah *si* sausage *ni* sausage *si ukule tu, nitalipa.*'

That's not the point.

You eat your *minji* in silence and wait for her to bring up the land-buying topic but she keeps getting interrupted by WhatsApp audio calls.

Finally, you tell her you are interested in a plot. Either in Ruai or Juja.

'Ah ah ah, Juja *hazinumuliki. Tuko na za Kamulu na Mailo Tisa.*

Mia nane 40 x 80.'

Imagine living in Maili Tisa.

Imagine getting up and finding your cat playing with a snake outside your door.

Imagine trying to get a clear network for a Zoom meeting in Maili Tisa.

Imagine.

A single Kenyan female living in a brick house in Maili Tisa with three cats, a dog, and a chicken.

Ata mimi si imagine. You have to be a widow or a single mother of three to pull that off.

So *waKim* adds you to a WhatsApp group with a very telling name. 'Manifesting Prime land ownership'.

You realize you are the latest member to arrive because people in the group are already exchanging dad jokes and such. Two days into the group you get the rhythm.

Someone sends a Bible verse at 5.00 a.m.

Another will send one of those positive mindset videos, with a pace that tells you they are made in PowerPoint, by a Gen X.

A too-long message with the benefits of eating green *hoho* before you sleep will be sent around 9:00 p.m. If not *hoho* it will be *mīchiiri* but it's mainly ginger and garlic.

Another post will be about why we should all stop eating meat right now, and by the time you get to the post that really matters, it feels like you have just stumbled onto Tuko or NairobiWire.

But Saturday is coming and you are actually looking forward to the plot-viewing trip in Maī Mahiū.

Part 2
One Chilly Morning

On Saturday morning someone asks if there is a dress code.

'Kwani ni baby shower *tunaenda.'* You laugh but you hope someone will respond.

One admin responds,

'Dress to explore.'

Saturday morning *mko pale* Kencom at 7:30 a.m.

You can tell who is going to check out the land.

Looking around at the men, everyone got the memo:

✓ Safari Boot

✓ Leather jackets

✓ Checked shirts

✓ Hats

The women also got their memo:

✓ Tight skirt suit

✓ Hair weave

✓ Painted nails

✓ Wedges, and other uncomfortable shoes

So I'm there in my khakis, backpack, canvas, and leather jacket, I think I will just stand here on this side with the men.

I don't actually look like a prospective land buyer here.

The transport comes. It's one of those fancy tour vans that have a place for your drink on the arm.

When you ride in one of those you start to know the answer to - Who owns Kenya?-

If you get a seat window then this is like going to America.

You sit by the window and look out condescendingly at people outside.

The pedestrians especially, just walking on the dust like that- who does that?-

As you enter the van you are handed a breakfast package

 ✓ One Afya juice

 ✓ One boiled egg

 ✓ One banana

 ✓ One brown bun

Quite healthy, to be honest. You had carried tea. So this works.

A feisty lady with a cream shift dress from Turkey, and nude wedges stands up and welcomes all, introduces herself then asks for someone to volunteer to pray for journey mercies.

No one offers.

So she points at one man close to the door.

Mr. John Kamau stands up and removes his hat then says the 'Our Lord's Prayer.'

It seems to satisfy all, the Catholics do a discreet sign of the cross, and all around there is the general understanding that this car, made by human hands, and driven by human hands, on roads made by humans, is now protected by the blood of Jesus.

The feisty lady says her name is Mrs. Wambua and gives a summary of the day's events.

She then says she needs to document this journey, and using her Infinix, takes about 35 pictures.

Pa, pa, pa, *mūgakīhūrwo mbica,* and they are sent to the WhatsApp group right away.

You start the journey, and some people know each other. So they are deep in business. It's a quiet hum until you reach

Uthiru *hapo* Nuclear. The van stops to pick up two women and a man. They are dressed heavily, with heavy scarves and boots. The man has one of those sweaters a wife buys a husband in Eastleigh when she goes to buy curtains.

After picking them up, Mrs. Wambua says we will play a game.

And she starts a rhyme.

'Ngai, no tūkūina?'

It goes like this:

Parachichi parachichi

Papai, papai

Tikitiki maji tikitiki maji

Aina za matunda

Aina za matunda

We are singing about fruits. Everyone seems happy to sing about avocados. And pawpaws and watermelons. Maybe they will be passing around seeds later for us to plant when we get our title deeds. Let's wait and see. *Huwezi jua* by the way...

Meanwhile,

I'm getting the hang of it. It could be worse. But sitting here in this tourist van- I could be going to Maasai Mara for a week. Nobody on the outside can guess.

In fact, they probably think we are going to Maasai Mara, so let me get comfortable in this seat and look like I just paid 16k for a holiday. My middle-class brain is feeling quite elated by this vain daydream.

Everybody knows that a group of Gen Xers and Millenials in a Van are not going to Maasai Mara, it's not even that direction! Oh well, we could be going to Lake Nakuru.

Lake Nakuru? To see birds?

Birds I can see on the farm when I go to shags?

Ati I pay money to go see birds?

Si ata afadhali I save and buy a motorbike and give it to someone to operate!

Or even buy a pump and start selling kerosene.

Everybody knows that these tour vans are rented for funerals. So we are probably going to a funeral.

That thought humbles me and I start to heartily repeat. *Tikitiki maji.*

This Mrs. Wambua is probably a school teacher. The excitement she has singing this fruit song.

You tilt your head a little when Tulaga passes by at a speed of slightly above 100 km per hour.

You shake your head to think that it's carrying people.

It has plastic shelves, a bed, a Skyplast tank, about three sofa sets on top of it, and green bananas.

Then she says it's time for introductions, and one needs to say something 'inspiring' to the group.

People stand up one by one, prefacing their greetings with

'God is good, all the time and all the time, God is good.'

I will probably start with a weak 'hae' and hope I don't start talking about my cat.

I am hoping by the time my turn comes I will have remembered a quote from the posters inside the 105 Super Metros I ride in. Something neutral and serious by Mandela or Maya Angelou.

I'm screening my brain but all it's giving me are reggae lyrics.

In fact, by the time the two people in the seat in front of me have had a go, there is a whole reggae concert in my head.

Coming straight from my heart

I hope you'll believe me

Until death do us part

This love will never end

You captivated me

The first time I saw you.

And, I cannot switch it off.

I panic a little and start to scribble a script in a notebook.

Lord have mercy if Mrs. Wambua does not positively kick me out of this bus at Maī Mahiū junction.

I check if I have fare to catch a Tulaga.

I might as well go to Nyahururu and explore my options.

Part 3

Cerebral Malaria Conversations

The woman sitting beside me seems like she wants to talk. But she doesn't want to take the responsibility of being the first to initiate conversation in case we don't rhyme.

But I can tell somehow *ameshani* summarize. I like it when people give me that look-over to determine how much my clothes and shoes are worth so they know what they are dealing with. The "am I better or are you better than me" look?

I know she is confused because my clothes say Toi Market but my hair says Adams Arcade. But I have also summarized her *na* from the look of things *ni mtu wa ka-fair*.

She has pimply skin but she has plastered a quarter tube of Fair and Lovely cream on her face and neck. If we become land-buying friends, I might mention she is better off ordering raw Ugandan Shea butter from me because at our age *manze...*

You need to nourish your skin before you start looking like a gunnysack. *Ti kwīmotaga o kīrīa wakorerera.*
Her big opportunity comes when a book is passed across for us to fill out our names and contacts.

She has noticed my email is a business name and she asks if I am a hairdresser. She doesn't ask it that way though, she asks if I plait hair.

I tell her, no, I don't plait hair. I lock hair.

'I'm a loctician.'

She gets interested.

She asks what I've done to my hair, and I tell her, 'These are locked twists.'

And start to explain, like I always have needed to explain since I could talk, why my hair is curly.

Whenever I have to explain it feels like, how you would need to explain why you have six fingers if you had six fingers.

She says she likes Sisterlocks but they are too expensive.

I don't really feel like discussing Math in the morning, so I tell her it's best to go with the style that you are comfortable with.

'*Lakini zinakaa poa.*' she says.

I ask her if she has a business or is in employment.

She works 'in finance'.

She tells me in the same manner you would tell your grandmother that Telegram is a messaging app when she overhears you mention Telegram and starts to say '*Haiya, bado watu wanatumia* telegram *siku hizi?*'

Before we reach Maī Mahiū junction, I already know that she actually has a car, her children go to private schools, her husband works in IT and this is their third plot they are buying with this Sacco.

'Do you buy them as investments or do you plan to develop them?' I humbly ask.

'*Acha nikwambie*! There is no better investment than land in Kenya!'

'How about political unrest, or maybe someone builds a big Church or Mosque, and on Fridays, you have to attend *kesha cha lazima* and every day, *mwathini* wakes you up at 3:00 a.m.'

'Ah! Those are not things to worry about. You get used after a while. And you can always lease the place.'

'That's my fear, if I build a house to live in, I will customize it to fit in with my lifestyle, and I would use the best building materials I can lay my hands on, as well as fittings and finishings. I cannot imagine having to give it up later.'

'So you'll never build?'

'I'd rather buy a complete house.'

'So why are you buying a plot?'

'I've just come to see.'

She looks away and probably is wondering why she even started this conversation because clearly, I'm not at her level.

'I want to give my children a secure future.' I decide to throw her some Big G, *atafunange*.

'Oh, *uko na watoto?*'

'*Ai, nani rika yangu hana mtoto.*'

I go on to tell her about my children.

I have three boys and a girl.

'*Haiya, na haukai!*'

I tell her I had them early. '*Niliona nifunge hiyo* chapter *mapema.*'

'By the way *inatakanga hivo, sio kuanza kulea wakati nguvu imeisha.*'

'(*Ma ma ma angīmenya ndīraunīria o mīringo īna na kinya dariri cia* boyfriend *gūtirī no anjīre ūūru.*)'

I am of course thinking of other people's children. The ones that wait for my curtains to open just a crack and they gather at the door waiting to swarm in. One has an injured toe and wants aloe vera, another wants to borrow a pencil, another one has switched on my desktop and is trying out passwords, and there is another one squatting on the floor with his palms together in front of him like a *muindi*. Another one has asked me three times if he can please eat the sim sim in the jar on my kitchen shelf. I'm pretending not to hear because first, I am still not sure if you should give people's children things to eat in Nairobi. *Kama ni kwetu* Endarasha it's okay *lakini hii* Nairobi *naeza jiletea kesi.* Another one is on the couch repairing his car toys made from toothpaste boxes.

Yes, these children.

They'll ask me questions like - Where are your children? Are they big? Do they come here? Are you very old? Is your cat a boy or a girl?

And sometimes I panic a bit when I think that if I had had kids when people were having them *ingīrī na kīmwana colleji. Ngai, rīu tūūngīīranagatīa?*

She tells me she will visit my salon one day. I tell her *karibu sana.* She looks like the kind of clientele I have. Nice people who come humbly and leave humbly.

Part 4

On the way to Maī mahiū

The man on my left has been trying to catch my eye, but I am not really up to socialising and he is annoying me by listening to our conversation. Why didn't he bring a book to read? *Ama aende tu Facebook?*

Anyway.

Finally, he taps me on the arm and asks.

'*Unakaa* familiar, *wewe ni wa* Endarasha?'

'*Ee.*' I respond, trying to make out the face.

(*Rīu nū ūyū ūramenya na ngūkīte gūkū* incognito?)

'*Wewe ni wa kule kwa yule kijana alikuwa anasimama* MCA?'

(*Woooi, gūtirī handū mūndū angīhitha* Kenya *Īno?*)

I say yes and ask which home he is from.

He thinks I am my mother's sister, I explain to him who I am and a light bulb goes up in his forehead.

'Ooo, ah, *we nīwe warwaraga marīria ma kūgūrūka!*'

He is excited to make the connection.

'*Na nīwahonire?*' He asks me if I recovered from the delirious Malaria and I want to ask him, 'Would I be here if I had not?' Instead, I asked him if he ever accompanied my uncle to the hospital to take me to the hospital at night.

He says no, but he was a doctor's aide then, and he was there when I was taken in with the Malaria.

Well, now that it's out there I feel compelled that indeed, I had delirious malaria (*marīrīa ma kūgūrūka*) when I was younger, once or twice.

But if we are to go into specifics let's say quite regularly.

Then I would start to 'see' things and scare the skin off everybody when I would point at '*Kanyamū*' there and there.

Kūbogotha. I think it translates to hallucinations or delirium. My aunts are saved, and they would get scared and say I was possessed. In fact, even now when I get slightly under the weather, I don't want to say it out loud in case there is an immediate need for a quick gathering to perform an exorcism, *kana manjohe mandware mathare*. My fever always comes with a bit of insanity.

I shouldn't speak so freely about insanity in case my younger cousins want to marry someday and the girl's family asks if there is insanity in the family and someone whispers,

"Gathoni *wao, rĩ, nĩ agũrũkaga, o na nokio atarĩ aahika.*"

And the in-laws deny the groom his wife.

But who is not certified mad in Kenya? If you start talking to people and go like,

"*Haiya, nĩwamenya niĩ nĩndĩndarwara marĩria mau ma kũgũrũka.*"

The other person will most definitely console you with,

'*Ah, ona Kimu witũ aakigũrũkite e* Form Three.'

"*Ngai, nĩkĩ? Nĩ Bangi?*

Ona tũtiũĩ , twamũiguire mabati igũrũ ũtukũ ũmwe tũkĩrara tũkĩmũhĩta."

"*Nĩmwamũnyitire?*"

'*Kũũ! Kaĩ atarĩ ngoma cia biũ, ĩĩ ndacokaga kũnyitĩrwo mũnanda- inĩ ahehete ta barafu.*'

"*Na nĩahonire rĩu kana mwamwĩkire atĩa?*"

'*Eee, tene na akĩhikania.*'

"*Hĩ, Ngai nĩmwega.*"

'*No onawakorwo ti bangi harĩ kĩndũ   anyuĩte makahĩtania.*'

"*Imwana irĩ maundũ maingĩ. Na ningĩ nĩ kũrĩ* second hand smoke."

He is a shortish man, light-skinned with untidy facial hair but the sort that's to smooth things over by leaving everything to God.

The kind who are only comfortable discussing the good old days, inflation, and how cloudy the day is until now because you would think by now the sky would have cleared a bit but look, you would think it's 6:00 a.m.

So our short catching-up moment runs out fast enough for me to start listening to the two people in front of us who are arguing whether this is the same road that goes to Naivasha or Limuru.

Mrs. Wambua has overheard the argument and she stands up to reassure us that since this will be our territory now, she will be sure to ask the driver to stop so she can show us the road that branches off to Limuru, and the one that continues to Gilgil. '*Ndio* next time *mkumbuke*.'

Part 5
'Kaba Gatīīri.'

There are two women at the back who have been in deep conversation, all going on Kirinyaga Kikuyu, so I have no idea what they are saying, apart from when they switch to English or Swahili. I turn around to have a look.

One of them has short hair and a black dress.

The other one has gold-coated earrings and tights.

The woman with short hair has no jewelry on her. Just the dress, a sweater, and leather shoes from Bata.

The kind of well-kept hair that tells you that this is a woman with wealth. Not rich, wealthy.

You can always tell.

In a country where 75% of the population is middle class (both upper and lower), the 10% wealthy are able to camouflage right in front of our eyes. We don't know what a wealthy person should look like so we either slap them up with the middle class while our eyes get bamboozled by the acrobatics of the rich, the new money, and the wash-wash.

Women of wealth keep their hair and nails short. Most likely it's because they will have a hobby like racehorse breeding and have to muck ruck every morning. Or they attend to their rare orchid every morning, those ones that you cannot work on with rubber gloves because they will wilt right away.

Us with little money are the ones running helter-skelter on Dubois Road to get the latest Brazilian hair and nail extensions.

A wealthy woman, quiet, but interspersing the conversation with direct questions like, 'What would be the biannual revenue generated by this processing unit a year from setting up?'

She reminds me of the day I was going to Karen, KSPCA, and two women got in. There was only one seat left, *hiyo ya konda,* one sat on it, while the other, a hefty woman with a round voluminous voice, sat in the crack.

'This is quite comfortable, I don't know why they refuse to sit here.'

'Ah, that crack needs someone who has eaten.'

The smaller woman wore open shoes and new tights, she had on a flowery blouse (Which I would wear as a dress) and beautiful earrings I could not stop staring at. I couldn't tell if they were real gold or dusted with a little gold dust that would fade in a month.

She was sitting in front of me while her friend sat in the crack beside me, but they were talking so she was facing backward all the way.

She had one of those skins that tell you, this woman knows how to take care of herself. It's not just about eating raw *hoho* and applying shea butter. This is a woman who has a five-step Nivea regiment, or the other one that keeps appearing on my YouTube feed with girls who have an accent. You know it, it's green.

You buy it at a wonderful price of KES 5, 999, or KES 6, 699.

I mean that kind of skin.

Her friend missed a few boils to be a boy child but she is trying, *ata ameshuka nywele.*

They are both drivers, I learn as the conversation goes on. The one with the blouse has invited her friend, Mso, for *nyama*, destination, Ngong.

'Aaah, I do not say no to things like these, it's not every day you get invited for lunch, *kwanza* on a Saturday like this *siwezi jifunga*.'

Mso is a really good driver, I soon learned. She has educated her children up to university on this job.

'This job just requires you to use your brain. *Wīra ūyū witū wendaga tu mūndū agīe hakiri, tondū nacio raha nī nyingī.* There are many opportunities for *sherehe* as a matatu driver.'

'It's true, you have a salary and at the end of the day you have something to do a bit of shopping.'

'Ee, even right now *si* I was called to reverse that *mat* and I got 30 bob. *Ona ingīiuga ndigūikūrūka ndinde haha ngīūngania mīthate hwainī itangīkīinūka ūtheri.*'

Mso's friend has something important to discuss. That is why they are going to Ngong. Some things you don't discuss *hapo* base *andū makīiguaga.*

Let's call her Wacuka, or, Waceera. A solid name that fits a woman who is in the taxi business.

Waceera has two taxis, and her son runs three garages.

'*Ngai Brayani nīguo a'arutire wīra na kīyo?*'

'*Īi we, ata ni vile staki kumharibu ningemfungulia ingine.*'

'*Aaa, ūcio kaī atarīguo ūgima. Īi ndiraririkana ūkīmūhingūrīra īrīa ya na harīa ndaraca- inī.*'

'*Īi, neyo nīyo yumīte icio igīrī.*'

'*Mwanake ūci waku nī angenia. Akaruta magūrū riko biū!*'

(Waceera has a son called Brian. She set up a garage for him, and he worked very hard now he has three garages. She would open another one for him, but she doesn't want to spoil him. Mso is impressed by this kind of maturity that has enabled Brian to multiply the investment.)

'Mso, I am thinking of buying a box.'

'*Ai, box nī gūtee.*'

'*Ndīrenda ya* long distance.'

'*Ona ti kaba wongerere taksi.*'

'*Ai, taxi ūtarī na ndereba mwīhokeku wakīumīra.*'

'*Wīra ūyū witū nī ūthūkīte mūno nī ūndū wa maguta. Ona hakīrī madamu ūrarutire box yake nuclear aramīrehe coria haha. Mūthenya ūyū tūraria ngari īyo īrainūkia ngiri.*'

'*Ngai! Maa?*'

'*Ma mayangai, na hīndī īyo nīarīhīire irima.*'

'*Nī ūndū wa maguta kana?*'

'*Kū! Kaī atarī madereba macio make.*'

'*Nīkīo ndīrenda twarie, ngūnengere.*'

'*No nii Wacera kuma ngwe nīwamenya nīndagūagūire.*'

'*Aaaca ndūkauge ūguo Mso, ndereba ndataraga magwa.*'

'*Ona nīnjīragwa hau nīndacokire chini hanini.*'

'*Ah, we ndwagīkoragwo wī roho juu.*'

'*Na ngoro īyo nīyo īndūrītie wīra inī ūyū.*'

'*Mùndù endaga kwĪyumia.*'

Waceera is thinking of expanding and has approached Mso to be the driver for her box. Box is a 14-sitter matatu.

Mso advises her not to buy a matatu because business has changed.
But Waceera is confident that Mso is the best fit for this.

Even though Mso had an accident and her matatu is still lying in a garage somewhere, her friend encourages her and tells her, as a driver you cannot stop driving because you had an accident. That's normal. 'A driver cannot count how many times he rolls over.'

'*Na ti kaba gatīīri?*' Mso suggests.

'*Ah, mburoti kūgūra ūtamībangīire nī ī komagia mbia.*'

'*Nawe rīu no ūkiugire* long distance, *no nīwamenya nīhagūbatara ikanga chap chap.*'

'*Ū ūrīa aathire kū na ndimwonaga rīu?*'

'*Ūū?*'

'*Nyagūthiī ūrīa warī wa kwanyu?*'

'*Ah! Kamagīra īyo. Ma reke ngwīre, nīūkūririkana Ūrīa, ka' hīnjīte! Na gaikaraga gekunanīire ta karaigua heho Kinya kwī na riūa, hakūhī kinya gaite rūta?*'

'*Ī?*'

(At this point I feel like they are describing me so I make myself very small so the story can continue.)

'*Ūmūthī ūyū ma ūngīona Nyagūthiī ndūngīmūmenya, agīire tūmakai, agīthakara, kinya akīerūha.*'

'*Nī wīra onire?*'

'*Ndereba ya turera!*'

'*Haiya nīerutire gūtwarithia?*'

'*Ona Ī ndarutagīrwa kīharo-inī kīrīa, nī Fredi,*' she points to the open space at Thogoto, just as we are getting into the bypass.

'*Nyagūthiī arutaga turera haha agatwara o gīthumo.*'

'*Hī, nama thīna nī umagwo.*'

Mso explains how that Nyagūthiī, who was not even a conductor, learned how to drive and now she drives big trailers (*Miguu kumi.*)

And how one day they even delivered a container to Kisumu together.

The plan is taking shape. If Mso will accept to be the driver, they need to find a woman conductor because, as she explains, it's all about the vibe. If you are going to sit in a matatu from here to Maua with a conductor she might as well be someone you like.

We are getting to the Karen Hub and I have a mind to add my fare and just get to Ng'ong to hear this whole story. I want to know what they decide. Is Waceera going to buy the box? Will Mso become the driver? And how is it that these women have been able to work hard and create their sources of income without relying on *Wababaz*? I haven't heard any mention of a man but I suspect the taxi lady has a husband. The way she talks, she is someone who is used to waiting her turn, knowing when to talk, when to press the right button, such speech cues that wives that have stayed in a marriage get to learn.

I get off the matatu and as I walk to my favorite *kibanda* for my fish and ugali, I am thinking about women's friendships.

How important Women's friendships are.

How women's friendships are like a piece of *mūteero* firewood on a cold July. You just need one, and it makes the other not-so-good pieces of firewood in your fireplace light up.

And how I appreciate the women in my life.

Because when everything somersaults your life, it's your women friends who will be there to tell you you need to go take a bath now.

Just ask Mary mother of Jesus. *Ni nani walikuwa na yeye hapo Yesu akikufa?*

Yes, John was there, but you would expect John to be there. *Huyo alikuwa na roho ingine ngumu.* Someone who can see all those visions in Revelation and not faint *sio mtu wa kuogopa ogopa.* So, yes there will be some Johns in your life too, but the women, treasure them!

So we went and arrived.

And it was anti-climax for me because when I imagine Maaī Mahiū, (I saw a Maaī Mahiū Boys High school bus yesterday so now I know the spelling.) I imagine it's a big open space of undeveloped land, with intermittent hot water springs. And I was even beginning to think of a business idea. Opening public hot baths *ta iria cia Njapani. No we nīūrona Mūūkenya mūgima aumīte o kūrīa ouma atī ooka gwīthamba?*

When we alighted, I immediately started to feel shortchanged because here we were, in a fenced-off area and I could see all the four corners.

'Is this it?' I asked myself.

It didn't look more than my grandmother's land and if this whole bus was expecting to get a share out of this, we would just be forming a slum here or another *Islii* if we built flats.

It occurred to me that, actually, I was the only one who seemed surprised.

I imagined the land we were going to see in Maaī Mahiū would be big enough to keep cows and sheep and plant tea.

Okay, maybe I was dreaming too much. But is it worth it if you can't open your door without touching your neighbour's nose?

Might I not be better off telling my landlord, from now on *acha sasa tupige hesabu ya* mortgage *mimi nikaange tu hapa* until it's time to be stashed away in an elderly people's home?

Am I living on planet Earth?

If I can't have a ranch I don't want.

Si uongo by the way. *Mimi nilirudi tuu* half-hearted. *Ata siku* sign *hizo forms zao na nikawaambia wanishukishe hapo* Kangemi *nikaenda kukula* melon.

Saa hii nataka mtu aniambie nitapata wapi simiti na 400/- niuzie hawa waChina huku Kinoo.

Part 6
Sirimon, Nanyuki

So my mother's cousin called me two weeks later and said, '*Ata kama hutanunua shamba, unaweza* lease. *Ata sio pesa mingi* six thousand *na unalima, kidogo kidogo umerudisha pesa yako.*'

'*Wapi huko?*' My interest is piqued. Six thousand I can spare.

'*Uko free lini twende?*'

We plan and one weekend we find ourselves in Timaū.

Timaū is a small town a few kilometres from Nanyuki Town. It's not as big as Nyeri town but it's more lively, maybe because it's surrounded by hills so the air is fresh.

On the way, we have seen big farms.

'Are these owned by banks?'

'No, no, they belong to individuals.'

'*Athūngū?*'

'*Aaca athūngū matirīmaga* broccoli *marīmaga nyamū.*

They combine their lands and call them reservations, then they get a few elephants and giraffes *magacihandīra nyeki.*

Then they make a camping site inside, and a few cottages, have you seen the planes flying about?'

'Yes.'

'Guests arrive by planes *sio* Uber. Then they organize marathons and such things that white people like. *Gūkū mahenya mokwagwo kinya nīandū a* Korea. *Nī ūraimagini mūndū ūtarī wona* giraffe *akimīona īriraxīte mūtitū īkīrīa tūhuti?*

'*Si analipa, hata kama ni milioni wanaitisha?*'

We stopped by one farm.

'All this is broccoli? You get a deal with a big hotel *kama* Serena, *unaweza uza sana*. Although most farmers here farm for export.' She goes on.

I say that maybe I could plant flowers.

She tells me those are fairy tales.

'Capital *yenyewe ni* million *kadhaa*. Flowers *sio mchezo*.

Piping the entire greenhouse, temperature control, digging for water, testing the soil PH, the fertilizers, and you haven't even sourced for the flower cuttings. *Alafu* pilots *wastrike na mzigo wako uko* airport. *Weh*! You would rather even plant tomatoes, and make tomato paste when you cannot sell.'

Then we drive back to Nanyuki and stop to drink *maziwa mala* somewhere.

And we meet my former editor. He is now dealing with land and we exchange contacts.

'So you quit publishing or what?' I ask.

'Aaai, editing journals is a dead trade. You sit there for a whole month and you still cannot even buy a reliable smartphone.'

'It looks good on a CV.'

'Certainly, but money is out here on the streets unless you are the manager of Safaricom.'

"I also gave it up, I am in personal services now."

'Business must be good, You look great.'

"It's a lot of work, but it pays. Cash *Kī mbakī* "

'Where are you based?'

"Nairobi, Mombasa road, bring your wife for hairstyling one day."

'Did you find a man?'

"Was I looking?"

'No, I mean, a woman like you should have a man, to even help with bills.'

"I am sure this is where our conversation ends, but nice to meet you again."

'I see you haven't changed.'

He says to salvage himself, 'Stay that way.'

2. Joy Bringers: Ndimia

It starts very innocently. Sunday afternoon you and your sisters are in the table room. You haven't even changed from your Sunday clothes, but everyone has commandeered a sofa, *mmejilaza tu* watching wedding show or, if it's 1994, you are checking out the piano guy on JOY Bringers. You wish you could grow your nails that long but with the daily *sufuria* scrubbing, you just tell your heart to calm down. One day, you will have a dishwasher and you will grow some nails.

Your younger brother is somewhere in the compound. You told him off because he kept asking questions.

One of your sisters has fallen asleep. Just then you hear your mother's voice. She is talking to *Wakefini* from across the ridge. They might be coming from prayers, *chama, itūūra, wìteithie,* or a water project meeting.

She sounds happy.

Of course, she is happy, a woman with grown-up daughters is blessed.

Grown-up daughters think of important things like clearing the table after lunch, preparing an evening tea and even getting the super started...

Your mother ushers *Wakefini* into the table room because that's where visitors are welcomed on Sundays.

She opens the door happily and sees the three of you *mwītabūrūkītie itīnī igūrū ta ndarabubwa.*

You see her face and panic and start to shake Millicent awake. She is the eldest and you want her to experience the wrath first. Your other sister scrabbles to pick up the plates.

Mother asks if you have been here all day.

It's a rhetorical question.

She tells her friend to sit at the dining table.

The thermos is on the table and she shakes it but the lid flies off because the last person didn't put it back on properly. She looks inside and the tea inside won't fill a cup.

'Where is Denny?'

You remember you last heard him chasing the calves from the fence but ignored him about an hour ago.
Or was it two? It's 7:54 p.m.

'Let me go get him.'

You offer, even though you have no idea where to start looking.
Your mother tells *Wakefini,*

"I won't promise you tea here, but let me put some milk for you in a bottle you will drink later."

You meet with the neighbour's kids on the way bringing Denny home.

They tell you that their mother said Denny should come home and put on a jacket.

Denny is shivering so you tell the kids to go home while you take Denny to the bath shelter behind the house and put a dirty jacket on him because he would rather be dirty than cold when your mother catches sight of him.

You also pick up your school sweaters from the fence.

Denny informs you that,

'*Tushau tulikula* sweater.'

Sure enough, when you get inside the house, you see that one of the sweaters has been chewed on. It's basically a one-arm sweater now.

'*Wololo*!'

Celestine exclaims when she sees her one-arm sweater.

Millicent says we need to hide it right away.

"We are already in trouble, we had better minimize it."

"But what will I wear tomorrow?"

Cele starts to whine.

"You can wear a home sweater under your jacket then at the parade you just remove both."

Mother comes back in.

She is holding her hands akimbo.

'Mum, *tushau tulikula* sweater.'

The boy from Ndūndūri offers.

'Why do you look like you live in a hole? Are there no clean clothes in this house?' She asks him but she is glaring at us.

Then she turns to Millicent.

The TV is switched off now and we are all thinking of all the things we haven't done. It's 7:30 p.m. and tomorrow is Monday.

You cringe, all of you.

'Are there even onions in this house?'

She herds the lot of you into the kitchen.

'*Yaaani yaaani* all of you big women, none of you has thought about supper?

Un Mon madongo unindo ka ogweyo ka ung'iyo wang' jowi to ok unyal paro tedo!'

She shakes the water containers and they are empty.

One of you dashes out with two.

Millicent grabs a touch to go get onions but remembers she is afraid of the dark so she comes back to pick Denny to accompany her but Mother, who is already spinning *ugali* on the meko says, '*Mtoto hatoki nje tena.*'

Millie looks at you pitifully so you agree to go with her to pick the onions from the farm.

You clean the onions outside and start to light the *jiko* outside.

Your father comes in and mumbles something to you as he goes to watch news or a political debate.

'Akinyi!'

He calls out. He always does. He wants someone to change the channel to Wan Luo.

3. The Cattle Dip Tour

My grandmother was summoned to school for a meeting with my class teacher.

I had written a letter to a boy.

She said nothing.

But the Saturday after we had closed school for the August holidays, my mother appeared.

She was told, '*Mwarīguo no ithako na ihīī gūtirī ūndū ūngī ahinyagia.*'

Your daughter is only good at monkeying with boys.

My mother got very worried.

So she told Tata Beth to "speak to the child before it's too late."

Tata Beth spoke to me. She said I needed to accept Jesus Christ as my personal saviour.

So I did by declaring in a church full of Kikuyu-speaking people in Umoja that my name is Gathoni daughter of so and so from Endarasha in Kieni West, *kwa mheshimiwa* Mūrūngarū and

I was a great great sinner, but on that day I had repented my sins and now I was saved.

I went back to school.

And the boy winked at me from across his end in the parade.

He was from Nairobi. Dandora Phase Five.

What do you do when a boy from Nairobi winks at you?

Si you just melt into goo and start coming up with lines to respond to the note you know will be passed to you by his cousin at break time?

The letter writing continued. Until my English teacher called me and asked what was that about me and a boy in class six. I had to explain. He asked to see my diary. He laughed. He was one of those cool teachers who just listened to you and made no judgment. Unless you were a real criminal then you got a real hiding.

****

I am not sure what kind of instinct parents have but one sunny Sunday morning, when I was in Form two I came to respect it.

It was 10:00 a.m. Me and my cousin were in a hole in the shamba sorting potato seedlings.

On an ordinary Sunday, our grandmother would have had us set off in our Sunday best and off to Church at 8 so we could be back by noon to go watch out for the baboons.

Generally, apart from milking and feeding the animals, we don't do manual labor on Sundays in Endarasha.

There is only one person who digs in his land but that one was accepted by the community a long time ago.

I was in form two and I had a boyfriend now.

'Mail' was flying from Nyeri High pa! pa! pa! To Bishop Gatimù and responses were going back pa! pa! pa! At the same speed. Every two weeks. The romance of the ages had been birthed.

Nobody born before us had been in love like that nor would ever there be another.

He wrote using a green biro and I wrote back in black with end credits in red. *We, tiga.*

And now he wanted to come home. Our home.

Plot 65, where I had a grandmother who breathed fire and a community that collectively approved or disapproved of any teenager's misbehavior.

Mimi nikamwabia ni sawa tu, we kuja utembee.

You want to visit? Come.

We set a date since we didn't have handphones then.

The story was that he was visiting my cousin who was in the same school because my teenage mind didn't think my *shosh* would know he was my guest.

He rode, 30km uphill from his home with a red bandana around his head. Like Sinbad.

We went to the same primary school with this young man and every Sunday our English teacher made everyone watch Sinbad for entertainment. I guess, maybe the boyfriend wanted to bring back memories shared in childhood in his favour but *ata sijui alikuwa anajisumbua kwa nini na nilikuwa nimeingia* box.

My uncle would later in the evening comment that he would like it to record the day Mike Tyson visited the family with a towel on his head.

It was bean harvesting season when everybody was around the homestead. One of those August holidays when a home becomes like a small shopping centre.

My cousin from Nyeri High was beating the beans, my aunt would be sifting them, then pulling the *chandarua* next to my grandmother to sort the beans.

My uncle would have his own *chandarua*, and some women, and children, and a guy who was just passing by would all be head bent over a pile of beans.

There were types of beans:

Mahūa, Gītuuru, Wairimū, Mai-ya-nyoni, and *Mwītemania.*

If you got a bunch of the last two it was smooth sailing because one is white, the other is reddish brown so you could sort them easily. If you got a mix of Wairimū and Nyayo (Mahūa), you asked someone to hold the gunia on one side, and then you shook it like you were washing carrots. The Nyayo would all come to the top and you scooped it out, the Wairimū would remain at the bottom coz it's tiny.

If Nyayo and Gītuuru mixed then *kwisha wewe, utashinda hapo.*

Nyayo is slightly smaller, it's red with white patches while the other is black maroon, shiny, and very slippery.

There was an aunt who had a young child and was busy fixing shelves and clotheslines near the fence. Interior decor and such.

In that kind of setting, I was in the perfect camouflage to start making *chapos* for my guest before I was found out and asked.

'Why are you cooking chapati at lunchtime? *Nī wīra wagire?* '

But of course, chapati being chapati as they are, cannot be cooked without them advertising to everyone "here we are being cooked" and I had barely put the pan on the fire when someone said,

'*Hī, na nīkūrī mūndū waigīrīra cabaci itūūra rīrī.*'

And my small cousin came busting into the kitchen and announced.

'*Nī* Gathoni!'

But before they could start asking why I was cooking chapati at this time, someone exclaimed that my other cousin had arrived.

'*Haiya! Walikuwa wanafunga Leo?* One aunt asked.

'*Heeee, ona e na mūgeni.*' Cũcũ said.

My cousin had closed school and had also brought her friend to visit.

'*Nīkīo cabaci irakīruguo!*' Shosh exclaimed.

And that's how I didn't get to explain myself.

I went on and served them one *chapo* each. We had barely breathed when my guest appeared.

My cousin recognized him and welcomed him and he was introduced and told to go sit.

'*Harīa methainī aheo gacai.*'

Such days were not common in Endarasha. Days when you are just around the homestead receiving visitors? Ai.

We are mostly out planting cabbages in the rain.

Or gathering soil around the potato plants - *gūthikīrīra.*

And when the sun comes out, even a bit, everyone picks huge up a bag or *kīondo*, and we begin moving manure from point A to point B. The cow shed would be divided into three sections so you swept around your section and then started to carry your manure. I preferred the wheelbarrow, it was faster and you had less cow dung dust down your back.

If your friend came to visit, you were both sent to do whichever work you were supposed to be doing.

Your friend would be carrying manure with you until midday, and then accompany you to the dairy. But even which friend would come and they had their own manure to deal with in their own homes!

Well, unless your friend was the child of a teacher and the teacher was practicing zero grazing and had a farm hand and such sorts of arrangements.

If you had a friend that lived in *gīshagi* (Gīshagi, are the settlements in the local town area where families can rent two single rooms, wooden. These are families where probably the father works as a cook in the local secondary school, and the mother will rent a quarter of an acre in Wasonyiro to cultivate onions for sale. Not where all of you tell me I am from. I'm from the countryside.) If you had such a friend, when you planned to visit them you would need to carry your small jembe, then decide where you would meet on Saturday *ūthiī ūkamarīmithie*.

I think that is why I feel such irritation when I see grown men here in Kiambu just sitting by the roadside *mang'ethetie*.

You cannot walk 500 meters without coming across three or five men just seated, chewing *miraa* and boring holes into every passerby. They annoy me, these men. They annoy me more when they pretend to set up a shop, selling (what's that snack kids like so much? *Ringoz*?). What serious man sells *Ringoz* by the roadside?

The men will even light a fire, by the roadside, and *magaikara hau mote*.

In Endarasha, men look like the wilderness. And it suits them, spending all waking hours being one with the soil. If you see a man walking leisurely on the main road, *huyo ni mgeni*. Even the ones who are employed walk briskly because they have to go and water the onion and beetroot beds before bringing in the flock.

A man with so much free time is suspicious.

Ama it's the proximity to Nairobi?

Capital city?

Kiamatawa?

And the knowledge that if things got hard one could walk to EPZ *na apewe kazi ya kukunja* jeans?

There is always the option of casual labouring *kwa muindi*, packing yoghourt, while the others wait for us *tukitoka* hustle *tūmanengenere mīcaara*.

When you visit us be ready for a comprehensive tour. We will give you a full account of how the cattle deep operates, and the dangers to look out for, the main one being your heifers taking off with another herd or leaving one of your young bulls inside the drying pen.

For me, I mainly went to the cattle dip to see the boys from Pura whom I never met elsewhere because they went to the IDD church.

I also went because I had a tough dog that would bark at any German Shepherd imitation dog and that made me feel like sort of a heroine in the lines of Wangù wa Makeri.

At the river, we would explain that

"Don't think it's just a stream, it can be very powerful."

Even though the time it flooded was in '95. But it never dries up, and just close to our home, we have a waterfall.

You must see the electric fence because we believe we would have been extinct by now if the electric fence had not been put up. It doesn't really keep animals in, if an elephant wants to take a stroll outside the forest it can. Have you ever seen the size of that animal?

So we took the guest on the tour and I went back home like the good girl I was to pick beans.

Now it was my turn to visit his home. The next holiday.

And that is how we found ourselves doing manual labour on a Sunday.

The letters had flown left, right, and north from Nyeri High to Ngandu and to Narumoro Girls.

At first, I had asked my cousin-brother to accompany me for the visit.

He profusely refused.

And for a good reason. I came to learn later that the form twos in his school had learned, through my boyfriend's visit, that my cousin had a sister and the boys wanted to know how much he wanted for both of us.

He had been told that he needed to calculate how many trays of eggs we would both cost, *aletewe*.

He had removed himself from that transaction and didn't want anything to do with any boyfriends trying to trade his sister and cousin for mere eggs.

So I asked my cousin-sister to take me. The deal was I would pay the fare since it was my trip anyway. I saved.

And this Sunday morning we were all set to go. We even got up early and tried to be helpful.

My grandmother was preparing herself to visit her relatives. (It was that time when she started to have misgivings about religion after she and some women formed a prayer group where they started to learn how to pray in tongues, but a more fastidious catholic woman had reported them to the father, and the prayer group was banned.)

The local Anglican Reverend saw potential in my *cũcũ* and recruited her to his Parish. You had to stand in front of the church and ask the congregation, 'Do you accept me to be a member of your church?' She did all that and learned a few hymns.

She liked one especially.

It went like this,

'*Jesũ we ũnyende, nĩngũũrĩra harĩ we.*'

(Jesus you love me I will seek refuge in you.)

My *cũcũ* would sing:

'*Jesũ we nĩngetwende, nĩngũrĩra harĩ we.*'

(Jesus I love you, I will cry to you.)

And I guess that is what makes sense to her because she still sings her version.

But she had barely learned to recite the apostles' creed before there was an all-out war in the new church and, depending on which side you were cheering, you quickly learned the lyrics to,

'*Nũkimanwo nĩkimanwo nandĩgatiganwo, o kinya Jesũ acoke.*'

(Beat each other up and don't stop until Jesus comes back.)

So, *Cũcũ*, in all her zealousness, decided, '*Aacha nikaekae hivyo sana.*'

And she spent her Sundays visiting different relatives, and when she came back on Monday she would be a lot more cheerful.

But in spite of her feelings about either church, she made us go. I, to the Anglican Church, and my cousin to the Catholic Church, our cousin-brother went to either.

So the utter shock of being assigned to manual labour on a Sunday morning was quite shocking.

She didn't say, 'I know you are planning to go and visit boys.'

She simply said, 'Go and sort potato seedlings in that hole, and don't go anywhere until all the potatoes are finished.'

Wueh!

If you have only interacted with potatoes in the form of chips *hakuna kitu unajua.*

If you have never packed potatoes into a *gunia*, life is still flowers and butterflies for you.

When you grab a pile of potatoes and roll them into a basket, the skin at the bottom of your nails peels. If you do this for half an hour, they start to bleed.

You keep doing this for an hour you get strips of skin hanging from each finger, they eventually fall off with friction.

But now you have to deal with the sweet sweet symphony of pain each time your hands come into contact with anything. Another potato, the *gunia*, your clothes.

You try to wash your hands and you are just now hopping with one foot wringing your hands and hating all potato-loving creations who cannot plant their own potatoes, dig them up, and pack them themselves.

Sasa afadhali those potatoes.

Potato seeds are another story.

There are three types of potatoes inside such a storage hole.

By the time you go to check on them they will have been there for a while so many of the seeds will be rotten. You throw the rotten ones upwards, out of the hole, a few will fall back and fall 'splat' on your head.

Then there are other tiny potatoes that have just been sitting there all this time, and nothing changed. They are still round and shiny. These can be used in mashing *mūkimo*. But you have to start peeling them three hours before they have to be cooked. They are called *tūbiri*. It helps if you have a really old grandmother who has long days, you just give her a basket of these, a knife, and a *sufuria* and she can be at it the whole day.

If you don't have an old relative just know they will be saved somewhere and pulled out when one of you needs to be pushed. And on a fair-weather Sunday afternoon, when everyone else has gone to look at cattle dips and road junctions and eat pawpaws *kwa kina* Wacuka Joy, you will be seated for three hours peeling a bucketful of *tūbiribiri*.

Potato seeds are medium-sized, shriveled, and sprouting. You have to handle these with care. Because of the sprouts, they are all meshed together. You dig up a batch and separate them one by one.

Then spread them out to dry on a *chandarua*. When they dry, you can now put them in a bag and take them to the house for storage.

That is what we were supposed to do this morning.

My uncle was to supervise.

The speed we did that job was nothing but record-breaking.

If there was a potato seed sorting competition, I am sure I would *Omanyala* it.

My uncle, seeing how hard we were going at it said we didn't have to bring in the seeds to the storehouse. Just leave them to dry properly. He also offered to watch out for the baboons in the afternoon.

That was just the best thing I had heard all year!

Since this was my trip, I had to heat the bathing water. It was already 11.30 a.m. so I took some Grade 1 firewood to light the fire.

Grade 1 firewood, where I come from, is from a tree called Mūteero. The area has so many, I mean, sorry, I rephrase. The area HAD so many of these trees that my primary school was called Mīteero Primary School.

I don't know the name in English. But we cut them all down and made fires after Independence.

So, Mūteero firewood is rare now and it can only be used to get the fire going when cooking important things like food or morning tea. You put one piece inside and add whatever low-grade firewood you have around. By no means can you use it to boil bath water regardless of the emergency ahead.

And here I was.

Using Mūteero to warm bathing water. For town people, it's like your mother coming home to find you boiling *githeri* on the gas cooker.

Or just your old self living in Nairobi and one day you decide you will cook *githeri* on your *meko* without a pressure cooker. And you are not the manager of BIDCO?

That is *Harakiri*.

In Endarasha, we shower with at least twenty liters of water.

If I'm going to remove my clothes outside in Endarasha, it best be worth it.

My cousin would carry that and still you'd hear him calling

'Kūi! Ndehera maī ma gwīkamūra na kabūyū!'

(Bring me some water in a jerrycan to rinse myself.)

So my uncle called him *kabūyū*, then *mbūyū* when he grew up.

He would just be standing there in the cold waiting for the rinsing water to be brought.

Which was quite smart because, by the time he finished taking his bath, if the rinsing water had just been there in the bath with him, it would be cold by then.

So anyway yeah,

I picked up some *tūmītero*,
Lit a fire quickly and we bathed and put on some trousers.
The problem with life on a farm is, when you have to go somewhere suddenly, that's when you realize *kumbe mwīrī nīugacaga.*
You try scrubbing your feet with a pumice stone, *wapi*? The cracks just stare at you like you just woke them up from sleep and now they are ready to rock and roll.
The only thing that helps is if you have been in gumboots, then your feet have retained their natural state but in this case, our hands?
Our hands refused to get clean.
We had potato stains.
And our nails had a nice layer of black cotton soil underneath. This, I started to remove with a stick when heading to the road but, of course, you cannot get the soil all out and even when you do, now your hands are dirty and you are wearing cream jeans so the probability of staining these as well was very high.

So you wonder *utaficha mikono wapi.*

And now this boy we were going to see, being a town boy, would not understand how you can have such dirty nails yet you claim to take a bath every day.

This was the kind of staining that would only be reversed by a whole day of washing clothes.

I said *haidhuru* in my heart. If he dumps me because of dirty fingernails *aende akaoe* model, *hata yeye asiniletee*, and told my cousin *twende tu.*

And it was a bit anticlimactic because, if you are 14 or 16 or even 18 years old, you have no business visiting a boy. You have no business sitting in the sitting room waiting for his mother to bring you mixed rice and tea. You are a child, and you should be at home scrubbing your mother's *sufurias*, not acting like a daughter-in-law.

It's also kinda deflating because you realize other people are just like you. They live in wooden houses and have family portraits in old glassless frames on the wall, hung up by nails. They have hotpots with no lids, and cups that would just love an overnight soak in conc. Jik. You are too young to be in a boy's home *shuwaly*. You should be with your girlfriends listening to K-Pop and taking selfies. In our case, we should have been home listening to radio, hoping they would play one song by Usher or Destiny's Child. Or listening to a Don Moen Cassette if we were good saved girls.

That's all I'm gonna say.

4. The Importance of Cows

Cows, where I come from, arc very important.
In order of importance,
The cows come second after the children born in the home.

> Then the chaff cutter
> The panga
> The milking salve
> The farm boy
> The sheep
> The dogs
> Others.

If you are just hanging about a dairy farm waiting for the heavens to open up, you are others.
At least in our plot 65, Mītero. The state of the cows can change the entire climate of the day.

I mean it. You might wake up to birds singing, and a medley of wildlife not too far.

You might even get out of bed at 5:15 a.m. singing,

Sisi wanangangala tumesema tuwamburudishe na hii ngoma but by the end of the day, you are humming Peter Kigia's *reke tumanwo* and you don't even wash your feet, you put on socks and get to bed at 7:15 p.m. and hope to try again tomorrow.

But before you sleep, you remember you didn't boil water for morning milking, and if you don't want to be shocked into a 4 a.m. wake-up call. You better get out and do the one thing you are responsible for.

You get up, put on your marvin cap and gumboots, and go back to the kitchen.

Your mother is cooking for the dogs, then boiling five litres of milk after, do you wait?

She is listening to death announcements on the radio.

Now that you have made yourself available, she asks you to bring in some water.

After the food and the milk have boiled, your mother says,

'Please, my dear little girl, could you bring me the *karai* for my feet?' You are in form three, so this dear little girl causes you to eye-roll but you get the *karai* anyway and pour her the hot water, then cool it for her.

You put the water boiler and decide you might as well eat.

You eat the *mukimo* in silence, now hard and dry. You pour yourself a cup of milk and start telling her about the girl at school who does too much shopping but still steals from people's lockers.

"What does she steal?"

'Pads, toilet paper.'

"Some people are like that. They want what you have, even when they have more than you."

'And better than you.'

Then you go to bed and get up for another day on the farm.

This is a true story: **A bloated cow, a fainted grandmother, and a happy ending.**

One Sunday evening, one of our dairy cows got into a fresh maize patch and overfed. Now she was bloated and nothing was working to relieve her.

I came out holding the paraffin and cooking fat that my uncle had sent me to get from the kitchen, only to find Aunt Beth *pale* against the lamp she was holding. She was bending over something that looked like a big *mũteero* log until I heard her whisper.

"*Nyina Nyakĩnyua...*"

My grandmother's still figure lay on the ground next to a pile of firewood. There was a knife beside her. I came forward and Aunt Beth let out another whisper.

"*Nyina Nyakĩnyua…?*"

'*Uuuuuu!*'

Our neighbour, who had appeared without any of us noticing and being dramatic, let out a yell, and she bent near my grandmother. I dropped the paraffin and *kasuku* and ran to the cowshed.

"*Mama! Mama!*"

I heard myself screaming.

'Where's the paraffin I sent you to get?'

"*Cũcũ* has fallen." I gasped.

And he leapt out of the shed and sped past me.

Nyakĩnoru, the cow, started to reverse out of the shed.

I ran back to the compound and found three adults and a boy half carrying, half dragging my unconscious grandmother. When she was laid on the bed, she breathed heavily and tried to get up.

"Mwangi! Ũ Mwangi?"

Outside, the local vet had arrived and uncle went out.

I went out to pick up the paraffin, what had remained of it, and the cooking fat and headed to the cowshed.

I stood watching the vet split open a young corn ear, pour some paraffin into it, and then rub it all over with cooking fat.

Kaĩ mwĩ na ageni? (Do you have guests?) The local vet asked when the neighbour's boy approached.

My uncle sniffed and stammered something.

"Mother of Nyakĩnyua had fallen," the boy said.

'*Atĩ agũa! Agũithio nĩkĩĩ?*

"*A, aca, anga nĩ rũkũ rwamũhĩnga,*" Mama smuffly answered.

I was sent back to the house.

'*A, ndwagĩtũmakia mũno.* ' (You made us worry) I found our neighbour telling the now awake fainter.

"I think I ran too fast to get the vet, so when I tripped over the firewood I passed out."

'*Nĩ ũũĩ ũrĩa Bethi akũmakĩte,* " (Beth was very worried) the neighbour continued.

"*Ngai, niĩ nyonire kahiũ ndamenya mũtumia nĩagĩĩtheecire.*" (Good Lord, I saw the knife and thought the woman had fallen on it)

We laughed nervously.

"*Inyuĩ, mhu, Nĩ gũtheka mũratheka? Kangĩhĩtirie gathiĩ ngoro mũngĩraria ingĩ.* " (Are you laughing? If it had gone into my heart you would be telling a different story) Grandmother said soberly.

'*Hĩ, kaĩ gũtirĩ itathekwo ĩĩ.* ' (Anything can be laughed about) The neighbour said.

"*Hodi*!"

The vet entered and seeing all was fine, informed us the cow was fine now.

"If a cow bloats at night I get very worried." Grandmother said then, turning to me and Aunt Beth said, "*Reherai andũ gatubia.*" (Bring the people some tea) "*Ngũmakĩĩte…*" (I was very scared) I said.

"*Ona niĩ ndiuma harĩa ndĩ,*" (Me too) Aunt Beth shivered.

And we laughed and cursed the blasted cow for breaking the fence and getting itself bloated.

After the COVID-19, drought came. There were news reports about cows dying and put in piles and the leaders were heard to say the cow owners should sell their cows when the price is right, to avoid huge losses.

It's one thing to see in the news, it's a whole different experience to see it live. We were driving towards Namanga and just past Kajiado we started to smell a very strong stench of rotting meat.

In my mind I thought maybe a dog got run over, but as we continued and the smell continued, I wondered just how many dog carcases it took to bring on such an odour.

And then, bam!

Looking to my left I saw about five metres high of dead cow carcasses.

I was gripped by something like a cramp in my stomach.

I felt completely weak.

And if that was not all, when I looked to my left side, I saw a Maasai herd boy standing in front of a very malnourished cow, barely able to stand. He was feeding it something from his hands, but I could see from the wobbly legs that that cow would soon join its family members on the ground.

There were carcasses upon carcasses, some lining up paths.

In the car, one of the girls said:

'Why can't these Maasais listen to the government and sell their cows? Why are they so attached to meaningless customs?'

Wueh!

I almost had a fit. But these were Nairobians, born and bred grown Kenyans.

They would never understand that a cow, to a Maasai, or a dairy farmer in the Highlands is not just a cash crop.

It's not an item you get rid of when its value depreciates.

I sat silent constantly gulping when we passed by another pile of dead animals.

Then I asked my friend sitting next to me-

"Your old car, the one you were attached to, when it grew old did you call the scrap metal people to come and cut it up and sell it as scrap?"

'Of course not. No! Why would I do that?'

"Why not, it's no longer useful."

'I sold it, it had depreciated but to sell it as scrap metal would be a bigger loss.'

She paused and then asked why I was asking about her car.

"Why do you say Maasai should sell their cattle when there's a draught?"

'What's the point of keeping animals you cannot feed?'

"It's not like that at all. When a dairy cow is no longer reproductive, there is only one more use for it. The slaughterhouse."

'Isn't that better than having them die in the fields like this?'

"Ideally yes. But a weak cow cannot make it to the slaughterhouse. It can only be butchered right there in your pen. Butchering a cow in the fields is an ugly business."

I explained to her how painful it is for a farmer to lose one cow. It's Nyameni, Munge, or Winrose that you are butchering. A cow that you have brought up from a calf.

When we would have rabies outbreaks in our area, it used to be the saddest time of the year.

Your chief appeared with two policemen with guns.
A vet was also present to confirm that indeed your Winrose had bite marks near the hoof.

The men would come and help you dig a grave for the cow, and the women came and made tea for everyone present, and then we sat sorrowfully beside the house. When the gunshots were fired, there was a big resounding silence, it was as if someone had taken grief and scattered it in the air. It was the oxygen. Even the trees were too shy to sway.

Neighbours would stay with the family the entire day, even helping to feed the remaining cows.

If no dairy cow was left, someone would offer a young expectant heifer to the home. This still happens. When the heifer gives birth, you get to benefit from the milk for several months and you can decide to keep the calf, for a price when you return the mother.

I remember one time two of our cows had to be shot.

Neighbours stayed with us the whole day, comforting us with positive words. '*Indo irī moko.*'

To mean that, as long as you continue working hard, you can always get more things.
Rabies was a scourge that could stop a whole community's activities. If a dog was spotted as having any signs of rabies, an alarm went out and the men went out to look for the dog and kill it.

To lose a healthy cow was unacceptable. To freely give up a famished cow? You don't. As a dairy farmer, you have pledged allegiance and commitment to your animals. You pledge to protect, care, and cater to their needs. Even when it doesn't rain for 12 months and there is nothing green in sight, you go to the farm and collect dry weeds and give your cows to chew on. Then you go to the river and fetch 200 litres of water and bring to them.

During one dry period, it got so bad that the only green left standing was the stinging nettle that grew as high as the public toilets in the open field of Endarasha market. *Hau kīhaaro.* One of my grandmothers would walk there, cut down a load of stinging nettle, and bring it home. Then she would cut it up and boil it in a big drum.

This water, she gave to her cows.

'*Bora tu ziweze kusimama.*'

As long as a cow can stand, it can wait for the rains.

Because that's the point. We as farmers are always waiting for the rain to come.

'If only the rains would come. The cows would be able to stand. We don't even want to milk them, we only want them to be strong.'

Because in the end, the rain always always comes.

Wakaratha

Wakaratha

Nī tūrathane nī tūrathane

Na wandatha na wandatha

Ngagūthīnjīra ngagūthīnjīra

Then something about sharpening the knives to poke the skies so that rain can fall

Nayo mbura nayo mbura

Ikameria Nyeki īkameria nyeki

Nayo nyeki, nayo nyeki īkarera njaū īkarera njaū.

So, here we were now and me feeling hurt that people could throw words like 'the Maasai need education' in the air.

I thought of the Maasai man, a 60-year-old who had done nothing else in his life.

And now he has lost his 50 cows.

What other livelihood does he know?

What would he fall back on?

Does anyone care about his mental health?

My uncle loses one cow and he cannot get up for a whole day. We actually have to make a trip home *tupeleke rabi rabi.*

How about 50, 100?

But people don't actually know how much a cow costs.

Do you know?

20k?

50k?

No.

A not-so-great cow can fetch you KES 120.

That's not much if you work in Nairobi and earn 250k a month but for a farmer out there in Ol Kolau, that is a fortune and the best response he can give you when you ask him why he is not selling his starving cows is. *Ndigithia-i.*

My friend said she had never considered it that way.

It rained a month later, and grass grew, and she texted to say that she hoped the cows would revive now that it had rained. My first convert.

And now, a year later there is an influx of maasai men, with limited Swahili, trying to sell belts, and sandals and wallets in Nairobi. From a herder to a hawker, how are they even coping?

Before we go on, arm yourself with these important family nouns

Mama - Uncle

Tata - Aunt

Cũcũ - Grandmother

Kasuku - A brand of cooking fat container that is usually recycled and used as a jug, bucket, milking jar, flower pot, everything. And everything plastic is a *kasuku*.

5. Washing Vyombo

I hate washing dishes.
Some people say doing dishes is therapeutic.
No, it's not. At least that is not how it plays in my mind. Actually, for me it's traumatising. I grew up on a dairy farm in Endarasha, where people don't drink water. They just keep drinking cups of tea the whole day. Using different cups.

When we get up, we drink last night's tea as we prepare to make morning tea.

At this point, we have managed to get six fifteens dirty even before 7:00 a.m.

Fifteen is a tin mug. Then the tea is ready at about 6:45 a.m. and we all grab a fifteen each.

There might be someone passing by, so let's say 10 cups.

When we finish drinking tea, some go to wait for the milk collecting truck, some go to feed the sheep, and some go farther into the farm to bring in napier grass for the cows.

Then I'll start to collect the dirty items.

Two *sufurias* that have had tea boiled in them, with a thick deposit of cream, three strainers, one was used to strain the milk. A plastic jug, two metal buckets, three aluminium kettles, the one from last night's sugar tea, one that had the *ndubia,* and the small one that someone used to scoop hot water from the big pot that perpetually has got water under the chimney. There will be two or three *sufurias* that were used to feed the calves, a plate that held some peels from *Cũcũ's* morning snack of sweet potatoes or arrowroot.

All the knives (the knives are always dirty) and the 16 fifteens.

Then on the left is a heavy *sufuria* that was used to cook for the dogs, and another one that is now very black because we overcooked the *sukuma wiki* last night, so it was dumped under a seat.

I'll pour water into this one to start soaking.

There will be about 27 dirty spoons, a fork, an egg beater, and a carrot grater.

I like to start with the cups so they can stop littering the work area.

Okay, let's do this together. You clean the cups *niiiicely,* then arrange them in the tin tray to dry. As you are about to start on the kettles, the person that went to "measure" the milk returns and deposits the *ngereni* next to the *sufurias*.

As a rule, the milk containers are washed separately with clean, hot water. (Although I cannot say much about how they do it in Kiambu, it's the first place I have seen milk being delivered in recycled Salit oil containers and soda bottles.)

So you rinse them and pour the milky water into the *sufuria* that had Ugali, this is the basis for the dog's evening meal.

You get more hot water, wash the *ngereni* and buckets, and rinse several times before carrying them to the fence. We hang them upside down on the bamboo sticks that make part of the fence. On the way, you drop the lids. You also drop the knives when carrying them to dry on the wire mesh rack.

You realise you forgot to wash the strainers, so you get more warm water and wash them separately. As you are washing, someone comes to visit *Cũcũ* so you pause to pour them some tea, and maybe bread and pancakes. You get back to your *sufurias*. As you scrub them, the black soot on their bottoms fills up the sink, if you are doing this inside the kitchen. Though it is much easier to wash them outside. You unblock the sink to let the water go and you see there are *sufuria* covers at the bottom of the sink. Three of them, and two metal plates.

You scrub the *sufurias* and the pan that was used for *mũkimo*. Then you pick up the cups and plates used by *Cũcũ* and her visitor. And the wooden spoon that is leaning on the wall. You wash these and clean up the sink.

Then your aunt comes from the *shamba* and deposits an empty kettle and three dirty cups into the sink – *ciĩna kinya tĩĩri*. All this before 10 O'clock, *anga gũkũ gwitũ tũtũũragio nĩ ndĩa na mahoya.*

At the same time, you are checking to see that the water level in the cow's drinking trough is alright. There is never a worse telling-off than when you forget to turn off the water and it spills into the cow's shed, and now the path to the milking path is a mixture of mud and dung. It's still halfway so you distract yourself with other things like sweeping the yard, getting some weeds for the rabbits, washing blankets, and then you pick up a basket and go to the area where they are digging up potatoes to pick up the cut ones – *mateme*. I get surprised when I go to the market and someone wants to sell me potatoes with cuts on them - *nũũ ũrakwendeirie mateme? Kaĩ andũ makorokire atĩa?*

You come back and start peeling them as you cook tea for the people working.

It has not yet been decided what is for lunch but that is beside the point, you always start cooking by peeling potatoes. *Haziwezi kosa kazi.*

The affairs of the day continue until about 5:00 p.m. when you panic, because you realise you haven't washed the milk buckets that were used for milking at 1:00 p.m.

You scuffle to pick up some dry leaves to start a small fire so you can heat water for milking and for cleaning the buckets before Mama comes in and you ask yourself *riu ngucuungitie kii muthenya*?

You hang up the buckets and *ngereni* and give yourself psych to wash the pile of utensils that has gathered from lunch. The scene is the same, the only thing that has changed is there is only one *ngereni, ga kiro inya*, which has milk from lunch milking. You empty the milk into a *sufuria* and wash the container. This might go on until about 6:00 p.m. You again pick up a basket and go to pick up potatoes, or spinach.

Not everyone takes their tea sitting down in this home, some have it on the go. At the verandah, you notice a cup on the shelf above the door to the left and another one on the window curtain box. There is a spoon that must have been lying there for two months. You will discover another one somewhere else tomorrow, *sikusema umemaliza kuokota*.

By the time you leave the big house, *metha-inĩ*, you have about six cups which you carry with your fingers in one hand like conductors carry your fare.

In the kitchen, you find the chicken jumping up and down the seats and two big ones pecking inside the dog's *sufuria*. When you say *xss! Umai mahuru maya!* They upset the *sufuria* and the contents are now on the floor, not helping anybody.

Mama comes in with his milking equipment and tells you.
'Aaaa, I forgot the small kettle where I was digging.'
He is not going to pick it. He is just informing you that you are one kettle and possibly two cups short and you better start walking to the farm near the farthest border before it gets dark. As for him, he is getting ready to have a beer and discuss politics *na hau Njogu–inĩ*.

When you come back, Tata has scolded the boys to bring the plates from their rooms. So there are plates from yesterday's breakfast all the way to today's lunch. When you get to the sink there are four plates, four cups, and four spoons. There's also a *ndung'u* - a larger fifteen.

There is no hot water at this time because the hot water has been used to start making supper. You shiver your way through Peter Kigia's songs to console yourself. When you are almost through, Tata brings you some warm water in a jug - at least you can clean off the sink nicely.

Tomorrow you will play repeat.

6. That Ka-age - Biashara

But why do you want to leave Kenya?

Kenya *nī īrī makua an mariūka*. (Kenya has deaths and resurrections.)

One day you are fired from that job you have been slaving at since you finished your Diploma at Kenya School of Professional Studies.

You worry about rent and fees for a month but then your aunt calls and tells you she knows where you can buy Crocs at wholesale.

'*Ūūke ūcite hau hanyu nja.*'

And people will buy, your neighbors will buy and you can post it on your high school *wozap* and get five orders by the end of the week.

Na kama sio Crocs, you and your friend from Kakamega do a collabo and hire a Probox.

Mūgathiī mūgakaihūria na minji na mīkohoro tō.

Then you come and park it near your local Fairmart Supermarket and by Sunday evening, *no mbia mūratara mūgĩitagĩra andũ anyu minji cia kũruga* because you have sold and made a profit and now you feel generous.

So your sister-in-law comes and you explain to her how *biashara inawapeleka,* so she tells you she wants in and, because she has a car, she says next time she will drive, and now *biashara* starts to pick up.

You even hire a man to help with sales, *hata unamnunulia* overcoat *ya* green.

Kidogo kidogo your brother-in-law asks if you would be interested in renting a room in one of his containers *pale* bypass. *Ata* he's not charging you for the first three months because, '*Naelewa hali.*'

So you go to have a look at the container *unapata, ah!* the former tenant was selling plastic flowers from China. When they were unable to pay rent, they left the flowers and told your brother-in-law *ajilipe nazo.*

Unaanza kuuza maua za China.

And because you know someone who does events, you tell them, 'What if I make a deal for the whole load?' The events' person comes and buys everything. And you give your landlord something small *gũcokia guoko.* Then you go to Gikomba and select those jeans *Uni* kids are wearing these days, *cihaana matangari na nĩ* camera.

You have a niece at JKUAT, so you send her some pictures and she shows them to her classmates.

Then she says, '*Si tufanye* shoot?'

Shoot *nĩ ngiri ithano.*

Wanaenda.

Then they make some TikTok videos.

By Friday *nguo zimeisha zote.*

So your husband says, 'By the way, *kwetu* job *wanadespose* pallets, *si uweke hapo kwa duka uuze.*'

You hire a pick-up, go to the industrial area, and come back with pallets.

And life continues, you know?

The thing I like about Kenyans, which is very different from the UK, is Kenyans always find a solution for everything - The Reverend Dad, *Mzungu Mwitu.*

7. The Village Wedding

I got invited to a wedding last week and I was thrilled because it doesn't happen often.

Usually, I see pictures one month after someone I know has wedded and come back from the wedding and someone shows me a picture saying,

'*Ona vile wanakaa poa kwa hii picha.*'

"*Haiya,* Jane *aliolewa, sikujua ata anadate!*"

I've heard that maybe they don't want to invite resident spinsters *wasiskie vibaya tondū tūtirī twagīa* people.

Valid point, valid point. But you know how a Kenyan will go on a trip to South Africa and come back, and then one day you see the photos on Facebook and you ask, 'Wow, how was it?'

But they just say, 'Oh, it was nice, very nice.'

And you ask, '*Nikiwa na thate k naeza nunua* ticket?'

And they bluetick you for a month.

So you ask, '*Na 50k?*'

Thinking now with 50k you will even eat at The Test Kitchen in Cape Town and stay at JW Marriott.

But they respond and say, 'You need more.'

And that's that. *Sasa* more *ni kama ngani sasa?*

And you, you just want to know, *niĩ nĩngauma* Kenya *kana ngũtũũra njoragia ohaha* Limuru *kwa mbĩra?*
Maybe they don't want you to think they have a lot of money.
Or maybe they don't want you to ask for their contacts in South Africa *usiende kuwasumbua.*

And me, I won't care if you tell me *ata* you didn't save for the trip, you just decided the previous week you feel like eating South African potatoes and you bought a ticket. Because, even if you have a lot of money, *si ni zako?*

But Kenyans have a way of being tight with information.

That's why someone won't even tell you there's an opening in their workplace when they know you have been looking for a job. And when you start a business they ask, '*Haiya, hizo vitu unauza zinakupatia* rent *na* food?'

And they won't even buy a single hairpin from you.

So being invited to this wedding made me very happy.
When you are closer to 40 than 20, all you want to do is see the bride coming down the aisle in a white gown, drink tea with other middle-aged women, and spend time with babies.

Being invited to drink tea for a baby that has been born, even if you don't have a baby, is also fine. I won't come there and feel bad when I think of the half-German babies I didn't give birth to 16 years ago. I'll just be waiting for your baby to smile at me. Then I can go home and hold my cat if I want to hold something, you know?

Other times I will be on the phone for hours with my home people about whether the rains will go longer or not and whether it is reasonable to plant the three months maize, or the six months maize so that the cows can have a regular feed. Whether to plant Rhodes grass or cabbage so that, if the rains stop, at least the cows can eat the cabbage.

But being invited to a wedding also depends on how you bring yourself.

Kūrĩ ũndũ mangĩrora moone. Ũyũ irio iria akũrĩa na weight *ya bahasha ĩrĩa agũka nayo harĩ na* discrepancy.

Ũhiki ndũthiagwo oo ũguo kĩmalala.

Even Jesus knew that. *Athiaga ũhiki ebangĩte.*

Gwetio ndibai akamarekeria na mītūngi, na ti KEG. Njīsū ndandiraga na kīgi.

Hīndī īyo ūthiīte na gakotoni ga tūkombe twa kaurū ūrareheirwo na Copia.

Kana kabahasha wīikītie matano ūkona ūgeretie mūno na mūtu ukirie kuma mana.

Those cups will be given to a cousin who lives in Pipeline, three months after the wedding.

Things seemed easier when I was a child. I'd see my aunts and mother and grandmother carefully thinking, '*Ū nyina Kinjo nī kīī atarī gwake?*'

Then they would decide that she definitely needed a new plastic jug or tray. (Trays were popular *kwanja cia mabati, ciagūragwo Kīgo* General Stores, Rware.)

Then they would look for a newspaper that had beautiful colors, like a Sunday Young Nation, and wrap the tray.

One of the best weddings I attended was when I was aged 13 or 14.

I was one of the girls in the line-up, the dress was a nice cream and black, not green or blue. The shoes fit, and it was just one beautiful happy wedding.

And Karuma, one of the sons of the wedding couple, said, 'The one who got us this coffee table must have known we really needed one.'

He always said such truths that made me laugh.

Weddings were simple things in my village.

If a teacher was marrying, we would go to that wedding.

We even were flower girls if the wedding was closer to home.

Everyone went.

The men served tea, and the women served *mūkimo* and cabbage. And the head cook served carrot pilau.

But there was drama.

My cūcū used to be an MC in the weddings, and between getting herself ready and getting me organised, something would drop.

At one wedding, the person sent to bring us socks came back without any explanation for my missing pair. So I was the girl without socks. It didn't help that the socks were red.

At another wedding, after I had been dressed, with a pre-fitted dress, and given my plastic flowers, a woman came and said, 'I want that dress.' She gave me her daughter's dress, which only went to my knees.

When my grandmother saw me, she felt very hurt that someone had had the guts to pull my dress off me because my guardian was not around. She later took the dress to a tailor to make it longer but that was the last we saw of it.

I guess that's about the time I started to understand that life wasn't going to be fair. That I would meet buck-toothed bullies who had more power than I had.

But I would need to learn to find my path and keep moving along.

Another wedding I remember was Mr. Ngamaū's. He was our headmaster for a few years.

Then he planned to have a wedding. One day during the parade he said: 'I have a wedding on Saturday, *na mūgoka inyuothe*!'

So we went.

Mr. Ngamaū was my all-time favourite headmaster. He came to school when he felt like it, and mostly when he was summoned to deal with bigger crimes. Like when the boys ran off *na kūu mū kuri kwa* Amos, to swim in the seasonal river that formed in the valley, and the girls followed to watch.

The girls would have joined too if their attire had allowed them. The boys would simply strip and dive in *kī India.* (😊 *Were they supposed to have been swimming like Indians? Hata mimi sijui.* 😊)

Swimming in the river was not against the school rules.

When you consider how far we went for cross-country races, going down to the river for a swim, after school, was one of the safer activities.

But the boys got carried away, and while the girls ran back to class when the bell rang, some boys were still swimming *kī India* in the river.

And so the following Wednesday, Mr. Ngamaū arrived, and the boys that had overstayed their swimming session lay in a straight row.

He swang and swang the cane and when one boy, having had enough for the day, tried to get up and run off, Mr. Ngamaù in his drumming voice declared,

'*Kīhīi gīkī ngūkūhura thanju inya cia njegeke ūmenye wī mūhūre we.*' And what might have been the entire school, peeping from the spaces in between the wooden walls burst out laughing, we knew we were in for it.

(But honestly, how was he going to cane the boy in his armpits? 😁*)*

I also liked him as our music teacher. We couldn't tell a crotchet from a quiver, but we knew what wind instruments, percussion, and stringed instruments were. We made them all, from wires and rabbit skins, bamboo sourced on Sunday evenings 10kms away from home, soda bottles washed out to get rid of the smell of kerosine, jars and cans and bottle tops charred in fire then flattened out to make shakers.

And when he came to class, we all went out to the field and played our instruments.

When he took the evening parade, he would start his speech in Kikuyu, then call out a random boy to come to the front and repeat what he had said in English.

If the boy couldn't, he was asked to lie down next to him until he finished his speech.

You had to be alert when he gave his speeches.

Else, you would be lying flat on the grass for several lessons.

What I remember of him is, he seemed to be having his own fun. He had a cheeky smile concealed in a serious exterior.

So you knew he wasn't carrying around a grudge for ending up as a teacher in a local public school and taking it out on the poor farmer's children. Him, he was just okay.

8. That Ka-age - Karūmbūsta

You are at that *ka-age* where if the heavens don't interfere you are a goner.

You know, that *ka-age* between 24 and 26 where you say, '*Bora nimekula na niko na pahali pa kulala, niko sawa.*'
Never mind that that place to sleep is in your mother's house and that food you are eating is the food your mother and father have earned, but here you are now, a whole adult, and the best you can do is run to the shop when your mother realises *hakuna chumvi*, so she goes into the bedroom and returns with 10 shillings and you take the ten shilling coin from her hand *na unaenda kununua chumvi ya* ten bob. You come back and show your mother the trending TikTok video then stretch yourself on the worn-out sofa by the balcony and continue the TikTok, Instagram, Twitter, and Facebook marathon.
You even comment on "The African Leading Men's group", giving advice to young men to think about the future, to think about their parents, and to work hard to build the nation. *Ūrī o hau gītī- inī wetereire irio ihīe ūrīe.*

But even if someone hit you with a mallet on your head you still would not get it. You think people are after you, *mahaters wanakutafuta*. You repost deep quotes from Steve Harvey and put on a facade of the oppressed.

Hĩndĩ ĩyo arũme arĩa angĩ no thimiti marambatia 7th floor Pipeline.

If you are a 26-year-old woman, the other women, 21-year-olds, are doing piece work in salons and packing matchsticks at MatchMasters. *We ũrio o hau ũkĩona Naija.* You even have a *Naija* accent, and you are not even someone's wife, *ati atalipa* rent *umlele watoto, weee uko tu.* Carrying around like a teenager.

Then your sister calls you one afternoon and says, '*Gĩtaũ ũmenye nĩũretĩirwo cibũ na mũtungatĩri.*'

'Why?'

'*Atĩ nĩkĩ? Kwani* you were growing dreadlocks thinking Mother would just sit and watch? The Reverend is coming to pray for you so that if you have joined Mũngiki, *uombewe uokoke. Pia* Chief is coming to find out if you are smoking bang. *Kama unavuta ujue utalala ndani.*'

'*Aaai Waithĩra niĩ itakĩrĩ mũrasta hizi dredi ni* hairstyle *tu,* uncolonize your mind *mi* sister.'

'*We menya ũrĩa ũgwĩka,* fellowship *ĩĩ kũu rũciũ.*'

'*Na kama nataka kuwa* DJ?'

You start.

'*Saa hio ni shida yako jua vile utawaconvince wasikunyoe.*'

'*Aaah mimi mtu haezi ninyoa na vile hii nywele imenikula pesa mingi.*'

'*Sema imetu... Imetukula pesa nyingi, na sikutumii pesa ingine ya* retouch.'

'*Usiseme hivyo* my sister, *mwana witũ ebu ata nimefikiria, unaeza nitumia* 600?'

'600 *ni ya?*'

'*Nataka kwenda kutembelea uncle, niliskia hajakuwa poa.*'

Ũgagĩtũmĩrwo.

Then you pack a small bag, dig up some carrots, and take a *matatu* to Kiamariga to see your uncle.

This is your mother's brother who is a very senior bachelor. He works as a lab assistant at a local secondary Day School.

A man set in his ways.

You know those men who seem to age like wood? By the time they hit forty *momīte ta mūbaū*, there isn't a drop of water left in them.

You don't know what these men are thinking, they mind their own business and expect you to mind your own.
They practice subsistence farming to avoid people coming through their homes whenever.

His farm has five lemon trees and a well-trimmed Kei Apple fence that even a chicken wouldn't go through it. The fence is interspersed with Aloe Vera plants.

He doesn't keep chicken.

He keeps rabbits. *Ciake cia kūrīa.*

And Bees.

He is the sort of chap who gets his tea directly from the Karirana tea factory in Kīrīa-inī. *Arehagīrwo kilo ithano na matatū cia 4NT akagīra hau* shopping center.

He buys salt in bulk, doesn't drink sugar, and uses homemade ghee to cook his food.

He even dries his own meat.
You go into the storehouse and see strips of dried goat and lamb meat, *ukarigwo kaī ndoka gīthīnjīro?*

The one thing he has always been ahead of is with his cooking gadgets. He had a two-burner gas in 1996. And only uses firewood to boil his bathing water.

He cooks his food using leeks because he read in his Food as Medicine Volume 3 (1995 Publishing) that leeks lower blood pressure, suppress acidity, and don't leave you with bad breath.

He might have married once in 1992 but the girl went to visit her aunt in Kinoo *akaolewa na Mluhya.*

You have always gotten along with this uncle, *ata* form four *alikutetea ukarudia kwa hiyo shule.*

So you have a history together.

The year you stayed at his house was the same year you discovered *kumbe* silent people have a life.

Your uncle makes wines and spirits right at home, but his best stash is the Acacia tree wine. The Acacia trees that decorate the fence are not mere decorations, my friend, they give pollen to his bees, and the sap, *we, wacha tu*!

Kumbe mūratina is not just made in Meru.

When you arrive, you go straight to the shamba to pick up leaves for the goats, and then you tie the sheep to different parts of the farm to continue grazing.

You know your uncle comes back at five sharp, so you bring in water and fill up the kitchen tank, then start to make some tea.

That's how comfortable you can get.
You know you will be safe here, your uncle is unquestioning.

No no ūrimū ūrakia tondū ūgūtūūra wīhithīte kwa mamaguo?

But it's that *ka-age,* a very sorry age, where one definitely needs rehab, because you act like you have inhaled something thick, and if something major doesn't happen to shake you to your senses, you will be 35 and still thinking people owe you. You cannot see, even when it's bright as day, that your life is your personal responsibility. That working hard to pay your way, and to take care of your parents, and your siblings is how life works.

That, sending money home doesn't mean you are paying back breast milk. It's what you should have been doing all along.

That your parents grow old.
And that if you are not careful, that parent might strain too much and one day fall apart.

And you'll wish you had made their load lighter.

Your uncle comes back around 4:00 p.m. but not alone.

Agoka na kīhiki.

Kīhiki gīthaka we.

And after introductions, he opens the sitting room and when you get in you see the windows have sheer curtains *za* yellow, *na itambaya cia itī ūkamenya baas! Mamaguo nīahikanirie.*

The woman busies herself in the very neat open kitchen right there in the living room. She makes tea masala, warms some *maandazi* in the microwave and serves you.

Gacagaca-inī īyo ukariganīrwo nī ūkūrugīte cai ūngī riko. But you say nothing because, in comparison, the tea you had made is akin to dishwater and should be thrown out. You don't even mention you had eaten eggs, you just keep picking up the *maandazi* because you are sure now those cannot even be called Maandazi, maybe they are *mahamri. Kwanyu mūtirugaga indo ya icio. Babaguo endaga kīndū gīkūmūhunia,* so your mother sticks to ugali and brown chapati. Such heavy things that hold the stomach together.

It turns out that your uncle, the one you assumed was cut from the same cloth *ya arūme arī angī a Kīeni no cebe cebeararīa haha,* and he seems quite at ease.

You are even sure supper will be spaghetti and minced meat.
You follow your uncle to the farm, he is impressed that you have fed the animals, the only thing you two do is to water the onion seedbeds.

He picks some strawberries from under a shaded nursery bed, gives you a handful and carries the rest home.

Getting back to the compound you can smell chapati.

He, now she is making chapati? You, in your knowledge, you know the dough for chapati needs to be made many hours ahead so the chapati can come out soft.

Your uncle goes in and gives her the strawberries.
Then you go out to the chicken house.

You had already collected the eggs, so you only add their water and clean out the feeding troughs.

You hear the woman calling out your uncle's name.

He calls him "Mat".

You almost laugh out loud because that your uncle, Wambugu Matthew (Uncle Mathayo) is now Mat.

Life is interesting.

Your new aunt, whom you learn is called Mary, is holding a jug of juice.

She pours for both of you, it's a banana strawberry yoghurt shake.

There's a plate of chapati.

Very, very soft chapati.

They even have pumpkins in them.

'When did she boil the pumpkin?'
But you know how it is with these big big women.
'*Ona mangĩkũrugĩra mboga ĩcamaga nyama.*'
Uncle Mat has obviously hit the jackpot.

Na nĩ ma nĩkaba gweterera Mwathani. 
You haven't discussed why you are here, but you know your lifespan here has been greatly reduced.

The following day you meet an old high school mate. He is now an expert tree logger and says he can teach you the trade. You think it's a good idea and even call your sister to see if she wants to partner in your new business venture which you will take back home.

'Hallo, my sister, *kana tũgũre karombosta ngũithagĩrie andu mĩtĩ?*'

'*Tiga ũrimũ Gĩtaũ, na ũinũke mami nĩaraunĩkire guoko.*'

The END

9. That Ka-age ~ Mũgeci

U memaliza University *vizuri.* Perhaps Egerton or Maseno. *Sasa umeingi*a Nairobi *kuandikwa* job *ukuwe* manager.

Three months later, you have got exactly one response from a company that is offering you an unpaid internship position and you are also required to bring your own laptop.

You tell your relative you have an interview and she gives you 300 bob. The interview is somewhere on Naivasha Road.

You google Naivasha Road.

Google tells you it's a road from Ngong Road towards Waiyaki Way. So you take a *matatu* to Ngong Road, drop off at Kona, and then get into a *mat* to Kawangware. *Wakinya Kawangware ũkora biũ.*

Somehow, *tondũ nĩ ũũĩ gũthoma*, you get to the interview at Ilri.

On your way home you are so hungry you decide to walk to Kona so that you can eat magnificent China on the way.

You get to town and queue for a whole hour. You get home and wash a few clothes and hope they will dry because you will need them tomorrow.

So you do the internship for three months, *o ūkīhoyaga* fare, and use your Toshiba laptop that weighs like a big rock and takes fifteen minutes to start.

Ama you get a job that requires you to commute to Mombasa Road, and you have to wear a suit.

You have looked around South B and South C areas and done quick maths to know that, if you are going to afford a roof over your head in those areas, you need a full genetic transplant where you get off that table as a Mohammed Abdul, fourth Generation Kenyan Somali.

The other option is to rent that one bedroom or servant's quarter but live on a diet of rice and green grams, never visit anyone that cannot be reached on foot and survive on one pair of shoes until the sole has a hole in it.

So you opt to keep your *kabedsitter* in Mwiki and commute every day, you can cross over to Mombasa Road through railway station *ūgaikūrūkīra hau Landmawe.*

One weekend, you wash your new three-piece suit using Ariel, *nīgui īnunge wega.*

Then you spread it on the low bush outside your house to dry so it doesn't stretch but when you get it off later, you realize something is extremely wrong.

Your 3, 500 Kenya Shillings sky blue suit is now baby blue and looks like something a teenager would wear to a dance-off Challenge.

Ūkamenya kweli maisha matirī rehearsal. You learn from your own mistakes and get on with it.

You decide if anyone has a problem with your suit, *wakununulie ingine.*

If you are a man, a promotion or a job offer might come sooner, because there is someone *mlisoma na yeye* and the uncle knows someone who knows someone at I & M Bank and somehow you get into the system.

You even wonder *kwani* what prayers were others praying that you weren't. And your cousin reminds you of that one day when you were asked to pray in 1993, your prayer had elicited giggles when you prayed, 'God help Moi and Kenyatta. And please take us to heaven soon.'

You thought Jesus would blow the trumpet before you got to high school, or at least before you got to Form 3 so you didn't have to do mock exams.

Your prayers are the problem.

You had not planned to live an adult life.

You hoped to be with the Lord judging the 12 tribes of Israel before you turned 15 years old. And here you are at 24 and paying adult bills.

Wueh!

And now you are 26 na hata girlfriend *huna*.

Apart from this girl Mugeci, who works at a children's home hoping to catch a *mzungu*.

And all she has got are a few German words.

You are not exactly sure what it is but whenever you see her, you hear the song,

"16 Calicos make one Madam".

It's not like she's *thaaaat* much older. *Ako thate lakini amejiweka vizuri, mtu hawezi* guess.

You met Mugeci at these weekend markets where your sister goes to sell her handmade earrings, she was manning (womaning?) a stand, selling gluten-free biscuits, made at the children's home to raise money.

That's how you met. You know that Mūgeci was eyeing the *jungus* coming to buy herbs and sour bread at these markets.

These ones are on the prowl for a fourth wife, preferably a slim-waisted-20-year-old African female.

But since you met, you are now almost a couple.

Mūgeci oona arī mūkūrū ndangīmenwo. She can hold a conversation in good English, *na mwatua kwaria Gīkūyū kinya thimo nīoī.* She also speaks Kiswahili and Sheng. She can also cook, though in terms of creativity, it doesn't make its presence felt often.

She can cook exactly three types of dishes very well: Ugali, with meat mixed in with spinach and *sukuma wiki*, White rice with a stew of *minji*, carrots, and big potatoes, and Chapati with a stew of beef, *minji*, grated carrots, big chunks of tomatoes and again, very many potatoes that overpower everything by sitting contentedly in the reddish-orange soup.

She wouldn't exactly ask you when you bring home pizza one evening, '*Īno nayo īrarīanīrio na ndūū.*' But you can tell she is having a hard time accepting that there is no real stew to go with the pizza. So now you have taken to making *kachumbari ya* avocado anytime you buy pizza.

Mūgeci is great, in terms of possessing all the makings of a woman, but there is something missing which you cannot really put a finger on.

One evening Mūgeci calls you and tells you, 'Please, please *nitumie* CV *yako kwa* WhatsApp."

'CV *yangu?*' You ask.

'*Eeh, nitumie kuna kajob kametokea hapa.*'

You decide there is no harm in humouring her and forward the CV.

She calls you ten minutes later to ask if you would be okay with moving to Eldama Ravine.

'*Kufanya nini?*'

'*Si hii* job *unaitiwa.*'

'*Kwani naitiwa* job?'

'*Hii ni* sure bet, *ngoja* email.'

You laugh.

But sure enough, you get an email notification to attend an interview at Career Point.

Ona itherū ūkegīra wīra.

Your girlfriend, whose highest qualification is a Project Management Certificate she did *hapo* Polytechnique *karibu na kwao,* has got you a very good position in a Pharmaceutical company.

Mūgathamīra mīena īno.

And because the expenses are few outside the city, *ūkagīa mbia biū.*

You even start thinking maybe you should even go to Africa as a Missionary, to give back.

Ama you are a girl and you have completed your Geology course *huko* Maasai Mara University and you enter this Nairobi *kutafuta.*

But everyone you know took a catering course and the jobs they are recommending include kitchen staff or server.

You say *haidhuru, nyūmba ti ya gūtindwo nī ya kūrarwo* and you start doing casual jobs in hotels *hapo* Upper Hill.
They pay you 700 bob per day.

But when you get home you wonder if you got paid because the tokens are singing and you offer to contribute, *wagītinda ithūkuma.*

Then your supervisor tells you not to come in those Ngoma Bata shoes again, they don't meet the Hotel's standard.

Now you have missed a weekend because gathering the money you need to buy a canvas shoe from Umoja Africa Shoe Company will take more than two days of serving tea and samosas to politicians.

And at work, they make fun of you and tell you, '*Si ulikataa kusoma,* enjoy your waitressing.'
You do your waitressing for about a year. And you wonder, is there a break in this life really?

You even start selling peanuts to your fellow staff.
And then one day your supervisor gives you some forms to fill, *ici cia gūthiī* Qatar.

Kimchezo tu you go for some interviews.

Up to that time, you think it's just another wild goose chase.

You don't even realise that you are filling up forms for Qatar Airways.

You even install Bolt and Uber apps, *o īrīa īgakinya mbele.*

Kumbe that French you did in primary school was useful.

Kidogo kidogo you are filling out other forms and doing more interviews and then you get training, and pretty soon you are in Qatar, but not the Qatar of 30k per month. The Qatar of working for an airline and getting enough pay to start considering buying a plot back home. Because that's what you were taught to believe in, that *mbia ingīkīria igana no igūrire ka* 50x100.

You can afford more but you ask around since you, you want land in Diani, the plot will have to wait.

Meanwhile, *ūgagīthomithia ciana cianyu, na ciana cia ciana cianyu.*

When you decide *aki* now it's my time. I need to settle down with a 29-year-old well-bred young man.

Have two or three *totos* and, you know, get your 30's right.
You will spend them going for baby showers, bridal showers and gender reveal parties. You will even have a nanny who teaches your kids to speak Kiswahili *ya* Kakamega.
So you start going out with various sons of Adam. There is one particular one, a lawyer, who is suave and makes big gestures like sending shopping to your mother and buying silk scarves for your aunts when he goes on trips to Oman.

You like him, but he can't get over his *Mercedez*.

He will bring it up in every conversation.

He works the M*ercedez* into your regular lunch with friends and it gets too obvious that this man is actually married to his car. If anything comes out of this, you will be forced to be *bibi* number two, no question about that.

Next, you meet Sam. Tall, Dark and Handsome Sammy. Sammy is *awright*, he even writes you poems. Until he starts borrowing money from you. Yeah, imagine he does!

He has a job and everything but he has a dependent trait, feeling that equality means a woman should pay the rent and school fees as well as a man can.

You were hoping to meet the tall, dark and handsome ones from Homabay and other Bays but here you are with Short Light-skinned and Average Paulo. (His mother calls him Faūlu)

You are in for a ride my girl. Brace yourself.

10. December Holidays

We are preparing to gather again somewhere, possibly in *shags*, where we will spend a lot of time comparing who has done better this year.

Who has money and cannot help anyone.

Who has no money and will probably need fare to get back to Narok, where they run a tailor's shop, doing repairs and crocheting *bocori* for nursery school kids, or PP1 and PP2 nowadays.

You wonder how they decided to move to Narok. Who picks up their bags and moves to Narok?

It's one of those weird cousins who have always seemed directionless, even after graduating from Kagumo Teachers, they were never able to find any real work. They just seem to wander this world.

Then there is your other cousin, the one whose mother ran away with a *mzungu* and you haven't heard of her since 1997.

His father remarried in '98 and moved to Busia, so he has just lived from one relative's house to another.

This time he doesn't come by *matatu*. He is driving a Probox Success.

Mworīrīria mūkaigua atwaragwa itūngūrū marigiti and he has even bought a plot in Ruai, *anajenga*.

There is a murmur when Yunī *wa* Tata arrives.

She arrives with one of those men who look anything between 25 and 45. *Kanda ciīho we itakūraga*. The sort that has been looking like retired Italian pilots since they hit puberty. They like to grow out their hair and beard and wear distressed linen trousers *na kablazer ka milaini ya* light blue.

They are quite a pair and they are already causing grins all around.

Yunī is those tiny girls who will never be referred to as plump or even beautiful. If this was a Jane Austen novel, she would be Lydia from Pride and Prejudice or Elizabeth from Persuasion. Very dark-skinned, bony fingers and a tendency to look like they are shivering all the time.

Austen would say, 'She was, at the age of nine and 20, a very plain older woman.'

And now here she has a boyfriend who is, light skin *hakuhī metanio na* Peter Kenneth. *Na kwao nī* Thogoto.

When the family gatherings and meetings are done, they drive to Nyeri, *makarara* Batian Grand Hotel.

Your brother arrives with his family of five packed in a small car, his three children and a Chinese man. The wife didn't come, she went to visit her family. *Inakuanga hivyo* by the way, *ata mlishazoea*. Your brother works for a garment production company. He is the delivery truck to the airport. *Nīkuo mamenyanīire na mūcaina ūyū*.

Some of the children in the compound are mesmerised and start to sing,

'Mzungu mzungu!'

Hung doesn't seem to mind.

He spends his days in short, green and yellow viscose cotton shorts with a Bob Marley print at the back. He stations himself right in the kitchen and says he will help to cook. *Kwao athuri nĩo marugaga.*

He has a small Bluetooth speaker which is permanently tuned to a reggae station.

Your grandmother tells you to ask him if those are songs from his country *ama ni zile za hapa, juu zinafanana.*

Your sister has also come.

Ekĩrĩte gakuo ka'ni!

You call her slay queen because *okaga na iratũ cia mĩkanye gĩcagi.*
She has these new nails they are calling acrylics, which you cannot even wash a cup without hurting yourself.

She was married in September, so they are still wrapped around each other and every conversation is punctuated with "my husband", *mũrĩ hakuhĩ gũtahĩka.*

So, they will be in the sitting room on their phones the whole time.

Matua kuma ũkerwo ũkamacarĩrie tari mote rĩũa.

That is, if you are the resident spinster who lives at home taking care of the

homestead or an elderly parent. If you are a man and single, you are transformed into a boy. *Kahĩĩ gagũtũmwo dukainĩ.* And the uncle who takes the children to the farm and helps them get plums from the trees.

If you are a teenager in that home, you wake up one morning and find your good shoes near the cow shed.
You know those Bata canvas that come in green with a red and white stripe on the side? I dunno what they are called. We used to call them *Ndina hunyũku.*

I honestly don't know any other name.

But if you had these shoes in primary school and wore them for a school trip, it meant you had made it in life. *Kĩmera nĩkĩamwĩtĩkĩrĩte.*

So your green Bata canvas, *irangĩtwo nahaha thutha Kinya kanyamũ kau komũ gakaunĩka.*

Cihũire mũtondo.

Someone from Nairobi woke up to see cows being milked and used your Sunday Best shoes as gumboots.

Ūgathirwo nī hinya. But you pick yourself up and take a bucket to scrub them.

You are singing, '*Wayunī reke hetūke na mūndū, ngacirīre kwa mūriū wa* Maria, *nyimitwo wetereri na mwīhoko...*' - Reke Hetuke na Mundu - Sam Kinuthia.

Baadaye your uncle arrives in a Noah.

He is more like a brother since he is one of those uncles who was in class five when you were in class one.

He lives along Kiambu Road but drives a Noah. He used to be an army man. He has three daughters. Heavy dark-skinned teenagers who speak in a *basso profundo*.

Your grandmother's friend has asked,

'*Nīa aya mararia ta athuri*?'

They go to schools where Music is not a lesson but a music course, schools where kids walk assuredly like they are CEOs on Wall Street.

Schools where the English language is taught by an Oxford Linguistics Graduate.

They not only learn spelling but they also learn intonation, pitch and poise.

So they have learned how to speak in a regulated voice and still command attention.

Not the mumbling we Kenyans do.

I didn't know we Kenyans mumble until I lived with an English teacher. And she kept telling me to stop mumbling.

'Mumble mumble.' I would say.

And she, sitting across from me, would ignore me.

'Mumble mumble mumble,' I'd continue.

She would continue typing on her desktop.

'Mumble?' I'd call her.

'Cecilia! You have to speak up!' She would answer, irritated.

'I'm mumble. ' I would apologize

And someone else met a Kenyan somewhere.

'Cecilia, we met a Kenyan and we had to really stand close to him and bend our ears to hear him. You Kenyans speak really softly.'

I got cured of it, the same way I got cured of sitting quietly in the corner only speaking when spoken to.

My Nigerian friend, a very introverted person, told me he was quiet around people when he was younger until someone he respected told him it wasn't cute.

Standing in a corner, mumbling, it's not cute.

Maybe we think it's a way to show humility.

I don't know.

But I got to hate it. And now I get quite bothered by mumblers.

Anyway. *Mamaguo ee haha na mandathi ma Vasillis*.

But you are told they are Called *Crozons* (croissants).

The girls have iPads and they decide to sit in the car until someone drags them into the house.

They will not eat anything that is not meat. *Na mandathi mau mao*. So you have been given one each, and those doughnuts that have chocolate or cream or sprinkles on top.

You eat them *fasta fasta* because you are 10 years old *na ndūgīte kīnyiria*. But when you look at the wrapping paper you almost choke because *ūcio akīrī mūtu wa cabaci kilo ng'ima*.

My uncle calls one kg of flour "*kamaithori*".

So, yes, that *crozo* is equal to a packet of *unga*.

Ugakiuga no sawa lakini kama ni mimi ningeulizwa hizo pesa tungenunua unga mingi sana hadi ya wimbi, but since you are not the one buying, you keep quiet and know that one day when people talk of *crozons,* you will be able to visualise what they mean.

There is your aunt who comes and brings her friend who has been part of this family since the two were in high school. You call her Maid *ya Mūhīndī*. She is not anyone's maid but has been running her own hustle, it's just the clothes she chooses to wear. She has always, for all the times you can remember, worn Indian clothes, the ones with baggy trousers. She even has a few *Kitenges* tailored in the same manner.

Shida niii, Punjabi suits have a reputation of being hand-me-downs from Indians to their house helps in Ngara.

So anyway, Maid *ya* Mūhīndī feels right at home here and in the evening there are talks about going to a Samidoh concert in Chaka town.

'Samidoh *no agīūke o haaaaha tūrī na twage gūthiī ndaci yake?*' Uncle *wa* Noah is psyched for the plan, and a few more jump in.

Even two other neighbours join in.

But you don't go because,
Ciana igūtigīrwo ūū.

There is also a *Kesha* that night and a few are going.
Some who don't fit in with either the Samidoh group but are not too religious either, or are just happy to stay at home, go to the locals and come back armed *na tuquarter twa* Hunters, Captain Morgan *na tūngī we hau tūtaramenyeka wega.*

If you want tea you drink tea, *wamejipanga.*

The following morning, as you are clearing dishes and taking them out to wash, you find one of the sheep chewing what looks like a flower paper.

You chase it to see what it is then you realise, *haiya*, the kitchen was left open and the contents of the bag that the aunt who came last had left in the kitchen, made a sheep's meal.
The paper that the sheep was munching was the final touches of a *Pembe* wheat flour.

There was also rice, you can tell, *ya kupima, tumafuta,* Eden tea, *na Marigū.*

Ooo!

That bag, it turns out, no one realised it was shopping and no one received it like the bags of Maathai were received.

Lakini ata yeye, why did she just leave the bag on the kitchen bench unattended?

The bananas must have been the goal the sheep were aiming for, the rice and *Pembe* wheat flour were just a bonus.

It's sad but quite hilarious.
You decide better to keep quiet about it so that no one is embarrassed.

Such moments happen often.
You think, 'Ah these village people don't know any good things.'

So you pass by the local cereals and buy them *Sindano, ama* Thailand rice. *Alafu* you get them two litres of Top Fry cooking oil.

Kumbe the season was good this year. They have sold cabbage or maize, or the coffee bonuses are out.

Now they shop at Copia.

Ugatūngana na kīSunflower oil *kīrīa kīnene hau riko*, the container is discoloured by smoke but you can see very well that that is Rinseed Sunflower oil. They also eat Sunrice rice. (*Nīguo wītagwo?*)

We na kīmūcere gīaku gia nyamakīma mūkarorana.
So it's just as well the sheep tried to drink the Top Fry oil.

But that is not always the case, someone may have really bought such a gift from the bottom of their wallet, and it is a bit heartbreaking when it is not received with joy and arranged in the wall unit like the rest of the shopping.

I'm just saying.

About bananas. You can know someone who came by public transport by the smell of bananas that engulfs them.

So on your way to Nyeri town, if you are sitting at the front of 2NK with the driver, you are basically riding in a personal car.
You can tell the driver to make various stops along the way.
The first one is usually at Kīangwacī, where you get your ripe bananas.

These you share out and keep some.

The driver may also get some.

If you are the other passenger sitting at the front and you don't buy anything, sometimes the driver will cut from his bunch and give some to you.

There are other stops along the way, but this one has been the most crucial.

The bananas are yellow and in various sizes.

You can get avocados, passion fruits, and sweet potatoes, but bananas always steal the show.

In less than five minutes, you are supposed to choose the best bananas from about 25 vendors.
It is overwhelmingly frantic.

It feels like, if you don't make the right decision and buy the finest bananas out of the 100 or so bunches being thrashed at your face, you will regret it for the rest of your life.

Your great-grandchildren will come to you while you are basking under a mango tree and they will ask, 'Maitū, what is the biggest regret you have in your life?'

You will shake your head slowly and sadly click your tongue in recollection of that trip from Tearoom to *Stage Ya Nyahururu*, 65 years ago.

'I only have one regret in this life. That one cold Friday afternoon, I picked *mūraru* instead of *kambara* bananas at Kīangwacī, I still don't know how I could have made such a mistake!'

After the *kondoo* has been slaughtered, and you are now roasting it *hapo inje kwa jiko*, the higher caste begins to arrive.

Makahūra honi mahingūrīrwo ihingo. (My bro assisted in writing this part.)

And because your home design wasn't originally designed to accommodate a drive-in. One of the boys is tasked with getting a wheelbarrow to go unpack the shopping.

Mūkabokera maratathi ma Maathai Supermakert *hurubarū inī.*

Oho hena tubagiti twa digestives (House of Manji) *na tūbaba twa* Creambell yoghurt. Empty ones, in a Maguna-andū supermarket bag. Those you take to the kitchen to burn.

In your anger and frustration about your shoes, you take three of the Broadway breads and hide them. *Mtakula usiku na* Bro.

(This is a true story. One holiday season when I was maybe in class 8 I was so frustrated by all the holiday stress I hid the pieces of bread).

So from there onwards.

You either:

    1.   Prepare to turn into a humble servant.

    2.   Run away. Call your *bestie* in Kīrīa-inī and tell them *unakuja na* 210 wheat flour, 4 packets.

But village people also have their ways and by December 28th they start to ask.

'Kaī ūrahetwo rūtha rūnene atīa?'

And you say you are expected on the 2nd but it's okay, you can leave on the 1st.

'It's better to go early *ona ūkīmenye gwaku kuhana atīa, usikue uliacha* taps *hivyo.*'

You don't get the hint and on the 1st you say you think your boss will understand if you go back on Monday, since the 2nd is a Friday anyway, *na huendagi* job *Sato.*

'*Aca we Waithīra mūndū ndendaga gūthaka na wīra.*'

You need to leave, *nīguo mahe ngūkū kīmūcere kīrīa.*

They also need to lock up some rooms so they don't have to think about cleaning them.

Ūkahe mūndū matano matano ūgecokera Nyairobi. You leave half-heartedly caring potatoes *na gakūnia ga bataraitha,* raw pawpaws, *makeruhīre mbere, minji,* spinach, *terere na tūcīmu.*

You come back to your plot and you notice life has been going on.

You even get the latest *mūcene.*

You already start wishing you were sleeping under a tree *kwenu* Kinangop, with only Merino sheep grazing by.

And it happens, whenever you come back from the village, you come back with your alter ego quite active.

You make resolutions and plan to be more healthy and proactive in your life.

You even join a Sacco and decide to start using spices in your food.

Wagūra mbagiti ya Royco cubes *ūkona ūgeretie mūno.*

And pretty soon it's March and life is going on.

Back to the reality of life in Nairobi.

You feel *kinda* sad sometimes because, in Nairobi, people are basically on their own.

In the village you have all these *ituura, wīthike, ka mūingī koyagīrīra ndīrī.* You can tell me what they are called in your village. These groups keep you in line. When someone dies, a timetable is quickly put up. There are people to go to that home in the morning and cook breakfast, people to make lunch and a group to cook for those that will come for prayers at 3:00 p.m. and on the day before the funeral, there is a group of women to cook tea for the gravediggers, and on the day of the funeral, there are people to make lunch, wash utensils and men to cook tea. The men always cook the tea.

If someone dies in your house, some neighbours may come with two Daima milk packets and one long brown bread.

That's it.

No support system.

Well, there is that WhatsApp group for your court where you basically just touch on, have you paid for security or someone packed in my spot, can they move their car immediately.

Such light matters that don't mean much.

If it's a graduation, they are not invited.

Where you now have a five-year-old and a seven-year-old and you realise that your aunt, the one you always thought was a scatterbrain, was not a scatterbrain after all, in fact, *alikuwa radar*.

She just needed to accommodate everyone.

And that is what you are now.

You are answering two questions asked by two children, you are serving a client and the handyman, who likes to come and see, *ni nani huyo ako kwako*, is at the door saying, '*Madamu, si unisaidie na karabūūi.*'

Karabūūi. Tondū nī kagoto ūhūraga.

So you tell him no, you don't have, but he hangs around talking to your children, who, for the snobs they are, look at him and continue to say,

'Mum, mum, mum, *mami*, mummy.'

You are, for now, keeping a level head, but if someone were to look you in the eye and ask how it's going, you would just start sobbing for 12 hours, *hadi upate kiu*.

Because one day you wake up with a toothache, the next day your child has chicken pox, the third day your phone gets into water, and when you are trying to save it, you knock over a kettle of hot water and now you are nursing a burn on your right arm, with aloe vera.

And your relatives call and inquire,

'*Lakini mko poa?*'

And you remark, '*Ah, sisi tuko poa kabisa!*'

Because you are in the city you know,

Nīwaumire gīcagi mathīna magīthira.

And you cannot stop thinking about the last time you went and passed your eyes around *ukaona* two, three-litre oil containers. *Rīrīa we, rīrīa ūgeretie mūno nī rīrīa warefill litre īmwe harīa ha mūgīthii*, Obama General Retailers.

You almost repacked the 2 kgs of Pembe *ngano* and Basmati you had shopped for them *ūcoke na cio*.

But because you trust in God, another year ends and you cannot explain how you made it, you just know it wasn't easy but you managed to be generous and keep sane.

11. *That Ka-age ~ Kuomoka*

Imagine *ūkagwīra kīwīra oguo kīega kīrī kinya na* per diem.

Kūndū ūratūmwo Marsabit *ūkaheo* hardship compensation.

You move out of your 4k Bedsitter in Zimmerman to be closer to work. You get a one-bedroom in Langata because now 18k *si pesa mingi.*

Ona itherū ūkagīa mbia, you order a fridge with two doors from House Wife's Paradise.

For the first time, you find out *kumbe* you can buy minced meat *na wasikuwekee mfupa.*

You are used to getting a big joint bone when you order 150 shillings of minced meat, which you stretch with onions and leeks and courgettes *na rīmwe kwīna ageni ūkagratīra makarati na waru igīrī cingīhe.*

Now you're eating meatballs for breakfast and shepherd's pies for dinner without even checking your *M-pesa* balance after paying for your shopping at Quickmart. You even buy eggs from the supermarket. Those that have a green label to show they are organic.

Then you decide drinking chocolate is not that great as a beverage.

You ask someone to take you to Kamukunji to buy a coffee maker. But after walking around you think, *aa mbona najisumbua? Si* you can get original ones from Amazon.

But since you have come all the way, you get some useless paraphernalia to decorate your bathroom. Those butterfly stickers and plastic flowers to hang by the window, and cheap bathroom mats with a Manchester United or Louis Vuitton branding which will start to fray on the edges after two washes.

You order the coffee maker from Amazon and, in order to make the kilograms count, you throw in some exercise equipment and a protein shake.

You stop drinking Ilara yoghurt and start on Delamere and soon enough you cannot have anything else in your fridge but Probiotic and Greek yoghurt. The one that comes in tiny containers. *Ūmīrīaga na gaciko kanini.* When the coffee maker arrives, you set out to look for coffee beans, they are not very cheap, and when you have that coffee once or twice, you notice that you are not really for that bitter taste and go back to Nescafe sachets in the morning.

By now you have even bought a full black forest cake from The Valentines and ate all of it in three days.

'Ah, the good life!'

You have tried the Java Menu and have had dinner at The Tribe, even Kempinsky *umeingia.*

Then you start sampling alcohol, there are different bottles of brandies and whiskeys and cheap-expensive wine under your kitchen sink.

Your double-door fridge has about four frozen chickens from Kenchic, Ham, Chicken sausages and chipolatas.

There is a big-size Thousand Islands salad dressing which you hardly use because, apart from *kachumbari,* salads are not really your thing.

On the upper counters you have big bottle of Braggs Apple Cider Vinegar, *no nī yakūremire nī gūcama ta matunda ma thakame maikaru.*

But when a visitor that doesn't drink alcohol comes, you offer to make them a vinegar and honey drink.

Your kitchen has many gadgets, even a real-life juicer that can juice pomegranates.

There are hot thermos cups in different shapes and sizes, some have your work label, most are your own collection and you interchange them. There's one for flavoured tea, one for black coffee, one for mixed coffee at work, another for hot water and yet another for *dawa,* which you only order from CJ's. The one with grapes.

When you have satisfied your basic needs you move on to making your house as comfortable as possible.

You even paint every wall/room a different colour, make some built-in shelves and change the toilet bowl. You order something solid in pleasant colours like baby pink and lilac, and you even change the tiles.

Then you rip off the window boxes from every window in your house and go to that street opposite City Market, near Jamia Mosque, where pigeons gather to eat grain. You get curtain rods and holders, then call a *fundi* to fit your windows with sheer curtains in dramatic colours, like orange and luminous green.

On weekends, you go window shopping on Ngong Road to get "quality furniture." You even pass by Otis de Furniture on Jogoo Road. You used to see it on your way to college when you lived with your aunt in Umoja 2. You used to wonder, *wale watu hununua hizi viti kwani wako na pesa ngapi?*

You don't buy them, but you smile when you realise you can afford them, *ni vile tu nyumba yako itajaa sana.* You opt for a custom-made L-shaped sofa and a lush carpet.

Then you are sent to Mali, you didn't even know Mali was a country that people go to.

You get to understand songs like:

'Abijan, *ti kūndū kūraya, no gūkū* Africa.'
Atakīrī kūraihu na Ethiopian Airways.
Wacoka ūkagūra kaMazda CX5. *Kumania na hau tutakuwa tukikuonea viu sasa.*

You even get yourself a wig. *Kawigi kega we kabrazilian* which makes you stop eating with your fingers.

But now your friends are letting you down when you tell them *mkutane* Habesha *wanakubluetick.*

Or they suggest funny stories like, 'Why don't we meet and cook pilau?'

Mtafanya house party *hadi saa ngapi*? One of them suggests you meet at Al Yusra *juu*

'at least *huko mnaweza* cost share *hiyo* Bariis Ishkukaris.'

Kumbe your former friends are broke. Na vile you used to think they had money!

Ni kuvaa tu wanajua.

You even start seeing someone.

Someone half-half who looks brown-black like a mix of Arab and African of the fourth generation, but he is from Ghana and speaks with a pidgin accent, *haidhuru.* He has a beard, and on weekends *ekīraga mariboko ma* yellow.

It's not something you would approve in a Kenyan man but *huwezi jua* life history *ya watu wa inchi za nje* so, *ukamūhe maitho tu.*

In any case, he is a gentleman.

He even picks you up and drops you home. *Si kukwambia mkutane* Kencom *ni kama mko* form two.

If you are a girl, your parents are happy for educating a girl.

If you are a boy you start thinking about marriage and settling down, starting a family and all of that.
And it's all good because life can be lived in different ways, and you are just beginning to bask in the sunshine of choice.

The End

12. The Land Cruiser

When I was growing up, the only powerful car I knew was a Land Cruiser. It was the four-wheel drive that would never get stuck in mud. We would hear its whistle at 4:00 a.m. and get ready to bring out the milk. It was mostly raining at this time.

So I would think to myself, "A car that can survive Endarasha weather must be the best car to have."

My dream car became a Land Cruiser, *ya gūkuaga mabebe na nyeki kuma Kīawara* to bring to my cattle.

The other Land Cruiser I got to ride in was owned by someone in the village. It was grey in colour, and the milk cooperative one was always white.

They had four other cars, *tucanter twa gūkua mboga*.

Because that's what made sense in a farming county.

You bought a car because of its capability.

How many *gunias* of potatoes would it carry from Charity? How many kilograms of onions would it be able to bring out from Kīnyaitī?

Kīnyaitī is a place in my village where, until today, the road is still a hit-and-miss ordeal, yet it produces the highest amount of red bulb onions, leeks and wheat.

You grew up knowing names like *Mercy Fagasson, pigoti* and *randrofer.*

Ti kūgūra gakari hau gatangīiganīra ngūnia inya cia karati.

People in my village had money.

They still do.

No niī itarī kanyamū.

So when I grew up, I would buy a Land Cruiser *ya kuumagīria mboga.* I would have land, cows and a bed and breakfast place where the tourists that come to The Aberdare Ranges would spend a night instead of paying a lot of money at The Tree Tops and The Ark.

And then I came to Nairobi and realised you actually needed money to develop land. And you also needed a lot of money to buy that Land Cruiser.

So I shrunk my dreams to fit my playing field.

And now the land and cattle I have accumulated so far is a small patch of potted plants outside my door, and a Tomcat that thinks I live in his house for free.

When you shrink your dreams you actually learn to live like that. You find yourself worrying about things like,

Na sasa ile avocado *nilibakisha usiku si nitapata imeharibika? Na ilikuwa ya* 30 bob.

Or sometimes I'm wondering,

Sasa vile Uhuru alienda retire, *kūrī mūndū ūmatwaragīra gashopping naarī maruge gatubia kana no heho maranyuo nīyo mena Mangī?*

But as you would have it, I am surrounded by people who dream big, people who even dream big for me.

Someone asked me the other day, *'Na mbona huna gari,* Cccilia?'

And I replied, 'By the way *sijui kwa nini sina.'*

Or this friend who tries to style me up, like inviting me for dinners at Art Caffe.

Nī ūrī wathiī handu ukona nama nama tiga nīundu mbeca itarī thoni ingīukaga guku o hwainī?

That's the feeling I get inside the Artcaffe next to the Stanley Hotel.

That is a place where you cannot go in jeans. You have to wear a white, pressed cotton shirt or a silk blouse.

Not that I get intimidated.

Ndacora kawanja haha na ka lipstick *ka* purple, *nīūguo. Hau hangī ngareka* sister locks *ciarie.*

The thing is, when I think of going out, I think of going to Rūirū, *na hau Tollo kuona Ndemu. Na kūrīa choma na kachumbari.*

Kana Karura forest *ngone mītī.*

When people go to *Parii, niī ndereciria ūrīa ingithiī* Kakamega forest, to see birds and butterflies.

When people are buying juicers and tabletop gas burners, me I'm just waiting *nifikishe* 15k *mshwari* loan limit, *thiī* South Coast *ngatubīre ngīrīaga* octopus *kūu iria inī.*

Then I come home and spend an hour trying to light a *jiko hagīre gītheri kīa mbembe nyūmū.*

I've often been asked, 'Why don't you buy a pressure cooker?'

Well, first, even if I had some cash lying around somewhere, I would not buy a pressure cooker.

Not that I enjoy this *makaa* business.

(*Anga ndikoragwo ndī mūgī biū.*)

I use the long division method.

Maybe that's why things move slower for me in life.

I don't feel the need to rush.

I don't have to cook *githeri* in one hour - *kaī arīkū ndīrathiī?* -

I was not always this calm. I was impatient and liked things to be done quickly.

COVID-19 came and told us, '*tulia, hakuna mahali unaenda.*'

The last three years have been my years of calm. I changed my pace.

I do things deliberately and with mindfulness.

I was explaining to someone that maybe that's the reason I've managed to plant not just succulents but also geraniums, roses and even bamboo.

I buy shelled peas because I want to hold the pods in my hands and feel the peas drop into a bowl one by one.

When I wash clothes, I sit on a low chair and gently rub collars and cuffs and feel grateful that I have warm clothes and beautiful tops.

When I brew tea, I turn the heat low so that the ginger sips into every water molecule, then I let the cardamoms, cloves and cinnamon dissolve slowly before adding milk, and tea leaves, and then wait until I can smell it.

When I cook, I make soul food.

It's nice to make food that looks beautiful in a picture, but I would rather sit in my kitchen and make soul food.

Food which starts to warm you from your toes up after a few bites.

Food that causes involuntary beads of sweat to appear on your brow.

One of the best experiences in my adult life was at my friend's *nyombo*. The night before the man and his entourage brought the cows running with tails up into the compound, one of her sisters and I sat behind the house marinating tilapia.

She would cut the fish horizontally, open them up then hand me the pieces to dip into the mixture of turmeric, curry powder, black pepper, cummin, dhania and grated garlic.

This was the fun part. We hung them on the barbed wire fence and stayed for a long time into the night shooing the dogs away.

If you have eaten tilapia that has been prepared for over twelve hours with ugali cooked over a wood fire, then you know it has the ability to knock you out right away.

Unless you are the groom *na hutaki kuchoma picha gwathoni aku* then you stay awake.

Several times I have poisoned myself trying to make fermented greens.

Have you ever eaten fermented green vegetables? Did you put some ghee on the side? Not ghee ya Brookside, ghee that is in a faded Coca-Cola bottle, with a maize comb stopper.

Soul food is not even supposed to taste that great. Like fried liver.

The best fried liver you will ever have is in Nanyuki, at Steve's Cabin.

The host made us fried *maini* for breakfast and we didn't need to eat anything else all the way back on the long train ride back to Nairobi.

Other Soul foods that I could add to this list are Kwaey Teo, a Chinese noodles and prawns dish, Malay Beef Redung, and Jamaican Chilli Concarne. You can add your favourites to the list and send me. Email *na* number *ni zile zile*.

Not food that gives you shivers as you eat. Salads and fries and hamburgers are pretty but my friend, *tinda o hau ūkīina "mūcere nī mwega, nī ūrīagwo na gīciko."*

So that you can cook *fasta fasta* and get to bed

I'm not rushing to my grave. *A a*. I'm taking as much time to savour every moment in life.

13. The Avocado Tree

I told my grandmother that I am now 40 years old and she said to me,

'*Tiga maheni ndangari ĩno kaĩ waciarĩtwo ri?*'

Ndangari is a tattered piece of cloth.

Cūcū is a very Christian woman greatly endowed with spicy language. So she started to sing to me a song about lies

'Lies are bad if you play around with them. They caused the sons of Eli to die in war and their father fell back on his seat and died, *we!*'

So I told her,

'*Nĩ sori*, I won't tell you any more lies but just know I'm very old.'

She asked me, '*Kwani* you had heard that there is a market for old people?'

Kwa barabara tu, andu makiiguaga.

We were going to visit Aunt Beth. Everybody calls her Tata Beth, even older people. Because Tata Beth will give you apples and avocados and carrots and, what's the English name for *kukumanga*? And everyone is welcome at her house, even women in serious stages of labour have delivered in her house since they couldn't get to the bus stop in time.

We decided to change the topic and talk about cows instead and some history, how she picked coffee as a girl, *kwa Mūnyeni. Mūnyeni* was a Colonial Lord, and that's how she met my grandfather.

When we got there, I went to look for Tata Beth near the Dam and she showed me a tree I used to know when I was a kid. We thought it might be an avocado tree but no one was sure because for years it had just stood there doing nothing.

It didn't flower nor did it look like it had any dreams of starting a family anytime soon.

It just stood there.

I think someone had even driven nails into it. There was a myth that if a tree was barren, you hit nails into the stem to wake it up. Who comes up with these theories? Well, that never seemed to have worked.

For years and years, that avocado tree stood next to the plum tree. Then there was a fence that needed reinforcing and some barbed wires were coiled around the old tree and we completely forgot about it.

If you asked me, I may have said it was just another fruitless tree like the ones we saw when we walked near the river.

And suddenly during COVID-19, the tree suddenly flowered, and started bearing oval avocados.

'*Haiya, Kīmūti kīrīa gītūire harīa mūgūnda kīina makorobia!*'

And they waited to see if the avocados would mature.

They did.

And it was the dog that delivered the first ripe avocado. He dropped the ripe avocado near Tata Beth when she was picking dirt from a tray of beans she was preparing to put on some *gītheri* to cook. So *wakagawana na ka-mbwa kake*.

(Finally, the mystery was solved when avocados around the farms and surrounding farms started flowering and bearing fruit. Our small bro, to clear his head during corona, had quit his job - a move we highly bent his ear for - and had started both fish farming and beekeeping. *Kumbe* it was the pollination from the bees that had activated the avocados. At least that's what he tells everyone who will listen. LOL.)

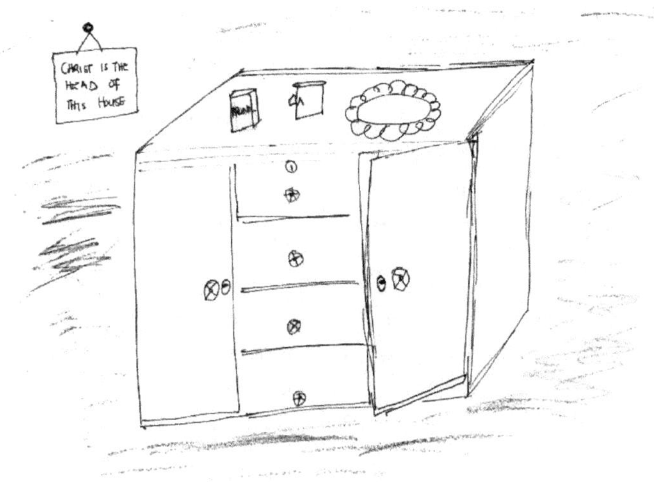

14. *Christ is the Head of this House*

When the Art teacher in my new school asked everyone who had this placard at home to raise their hands, it was only me and another boy who had their hands down.

Then she moved on to ask,

'If you have a sideboard at home raise your hands.'

The entire class raised their hands.

My hand was still down.

So she went on to describe what a sideboard was, in most homes, it is a centrepiece.

I thought about our kitchen cupboard.

It really didn't qualify.

Kĩarĩ gĩtiroo oroũguo kĩairĩtio ni ndogo (What's the word for soot? *Mũũrarũ,* or that's a type of snake?)

My uncle had put together that cupboard with bits and pieces of off-cuts.

It served the purpose, but it wasn't a centrepiece.

The "Jesus" placard was popular in other homes that were different from mine.

Twakoragwo mīciī inī ya andú mebangīte we.

People who cooked chapati in the living room while watching Vioja Mahakamani.

People who cooked stew for *mūkimo*.

Because, if Jesus was the unseen guest at every meal, *si basi* one had to make an impression?

Christ is the Head of this House.

The unseen Guest at every meal.

The silent listener to every prayer?

It worked as a CCTV too for the parents. If Jesus was watching and listening, then you couldn't misbehave in the house.

You would take your misdemeanours *huko mbaaliii karibu na fence penye Yesu haoni.*

I didn't know how true the words of this blue-coloured plaque would take meaning in my later life.

Thirty-plus years later, Christ is still the head of this house.

And from the look of things, it's gonna stay that way.

Mūrarī - that's the word for soot.

Everything in our kitchen was covered in soot.

Even the formerly purple jug had black trimmings.

When it rained and you were cooking tea, if you turned around you would get very confused because,

"When did I throw in tea leaves?"

When you started to sieve the tea you would see, *ah, kumbe nī mūrarī.*

Which was okay anyway.

Soot was a type of old woman's medicine.

If your chicken started to fall asleep while standing, in the middle of the day, not sleeping like sleeping with dreams, *kusinzia kama mtu amekula ugali saa saba kinya agaita rūta rī...*

Then you would mix a bit of soot with their drinking water.

They would be awake in no time.

It probably has caffeine.

I don't know.

I don't know if it has been tried on humans.

The only things that didn't get stained by soot were the kettles and tin cups.

We used tin cups and plates and everything else is aluminium or silver.

So when someone is washing utensils, it sounds like Kosovo.

If someone is washing utensils and singing songs by George Wanjaro, then it sounds like Kosovo and Herzegovina. Even the dogs start to bark.

And the chickens, seeing an opportunity, would come and get into the *sufuria ya Ugali* that was soaking by the side.

If it had rained before you took the utensils out, the *ugali sufuria* turns brown and black.

When you try to tell the chicken:

'*Schuu! Schu! Thiĩi managĩ maya!*'

They jump into the basin that has the rinsed cups and then step on the milk containers.

So now you have chicken footprints all over the scene.

If someone is trying to access the homestead, *no aikirie mahiga aiguuuo.*

You ask yourself, *kaĩ ũtangĩaciariĩrũo Londoni wonagĩrĩ ngũkũ mũkawa inĩ?*

Ona ũkamba kũhoria karendio nĩ kũigua pressure *ĩkĩambatĩra.*

Your brother is not around, *aguthiĩte Muiga kuona* Safari Rally, meaning after this you are going to take a rope and sack to go and bring in the evening napier grass. *Ũkaboeka harĩa ũgũtigairie.*

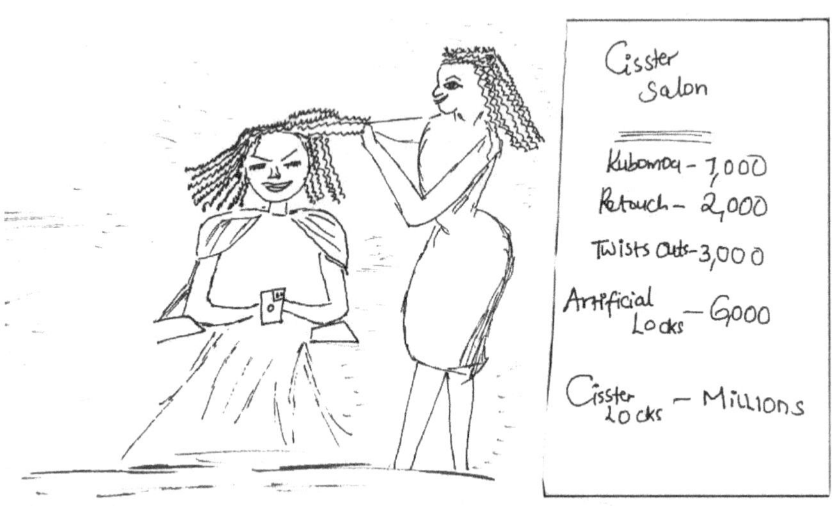

15. The Salon Caste System

When all else refused to work, I decided to learn how to plait people's hair. After all, I am in Africa. Women, and even men will always want their hair plaited, locked, shaved or styled. It's actually the best camouflage for a writer I'd say. When I tell people I am a hairdresser, they dismiss me and think - *Ah, huyu hakuna kitu anajua* - they become very open and are ready to tell you anything because, *ah, mtu wa* salon *anasikiliza watu wengi, hata hawezi* record. It's true. We listen to many people, even when we don't want to. But it has been such a fun ride. I have worked with awesome professionals, and met really cool clients who appreciate that what I am offering is a personal service which you should do for yourself but, because I am trained and you don't have the time to go and get the training, so, you respect my work, I respect your money.

If I could write a book about the different clientele that I meet, I would need a lot of money to get the publishing done. Maybe I will, but for now, let's peek inside the salon.

At the top of the pack is the Salon Owner, or Owners. These don't really have a position. They only come around to check on things and ensure bills are paid.

1. The Hairdresser

These are the kings and queens in a busy salon and they answer directly to the salon owner. At times the salon owners may also be involved in the hairdressing activities. They may have over 200 clients. Clients will come directly to them and then get the service, or be assigned the most qualified and experienced hairdresser.

One thing I've noticed since I got into the Salon Space is the shift that happens in some people's minds when they have an upper hand.

They see the servant-master relationship and nothing else. Someone will hear that you are a hairdresser and will think they can just call you up in the morning so that you can run to their house in Matasia to do their hair. Since that's what you do, with no regard for prior bookings.

If you are starting out, you may find yourself running about trying to please every new client. But you eventually have to create a system where everyone is served by order of first come first served. It is also very okay to let go of a client who doesn't respect their appointments or complains too much about everything.

Yet, there is an elite class of clients, which I am glad to have, who know that my Salon business is a business. They book early in advance, follow the advice they get concerning hair and skin care, are pleasant and nice, and don't bargain too much. These are my VIP clients.

2. *Kinyozi* (If the *kinyozi* cuts hair and also does locks and sister locks then he is at par with the hairdressers).

3. The Salon Manager

(She will make the bookings and manage the running of the salon, but she has to be really polite to the hairdressers else she can lose her position very fast). But to any other person in a salon, the Salon Manager is the one who determines whether you will have a good day or a bad one. She should be a snobby, possibly thin and dark-skinned Catholic-raised girl who will wear skirt suits and long *Kong Kongs* from Kamukunji. She draws her own eyebrows, with a black eye pencil, straight out like girls from Karatina. The salon owner trusts her with accounts because she will even work Sundays if need be.

4. Masseuse

Depending on the salon, sometimes the Masseuse, if she does skin care and consultations, will be number three.

She is respected because one of her clients can easily pay one week of the salon's bills. Someone coming in for a massage will obviously bring a plus one. They will probably end up doing nails and eyebrows, they will even buy skincare treatments and oils from the salon's shop before they leave.

5. Sink Person/Shampoo Boy.

If you are a hairdresser, you must have a peaceful working relationship because this is where it all starts or ends. The shampoo boy can calm down an angry client so they are manageable by the time they get to you, or they can ensure enough water gets into the client's ears to make them deaf for a few hours. Your client will be so exhausted by the time they get you, nothing you do will change anything. Then the Shampoo Boy will put the dryer on too high and hit the client's forehead on the dryer's lid and all he will keep saying is sorry.

6. Hair Dresser's Assistant

This one has a real *cheo*. She has skills as good as the hairdresser, but due to age or other circumstances, she may not have established her own clientele base, so she relies on the hairdresser's clients. At times she will even work on an entire head by herself and the client won't feel short-changed. A hairdresser's assistant gets all the perks of a hairdresser's benefits without the pressure of paying for a working station. She is also available to do other jobs around the salon when her hairdresser is not around.

7. The Receptionist.

This one ushers in clients but has no real power, she might be a make-up artist or be used as the social media person in the salon. And all content will go up with captions like: 'Trust us with Your hair every day.'

But a receptionist can break or make your salon's image. If she behaves like a typical M-Pesa lady, then you'll never know how many walk-ins walked out as soon as she opened her mouth. Please instruct your receptionist not to eat at the reception. Allow them a five-minute break to go and eat their microwaved *matoke* somewhere else.

There is no bigger put-off than walking into a salon to have a skin treatment service and the first thing that reaches your nose is the smell of a reheated *minji* and tomato stew.

8. Nail Technician.

These are the slay queens and kings in any salon. They don't even have to have any clients, they just flirt with any client who comes in to have their hair done na *wanawaingiza* box. They don't sweat the small stuff, in fact, in my observation, they are the happiest in the salon.

9. The Messenger

The Messenger can be a man or a woman, their job is to take the blow dryer to the fundi when it stops working, s/he is also responsible for deliveries into the salon. If it's a dude, you will find him going up the stairs with 20 litres of refilled drinking water on his shoulders or, conversely, a 20-litre shampoo *mtungi*. The good thing about being a messenger is you are not really intimate with the salon drama. You don't even have to be in the salon at all times, just be around there somewhere using the free wifi to watch TikTok videos.

10. The Intern

The intern comes with a recommendation letter from Ashleys or Pivot Point, he will get some respect. He will even be allowed to hover around a client so that he can learn a new style. An intern hopes to eventually work in the salon he is attached to, but since he is not paying bills in many instances, he can be laid back and nonchalant and the salon owner will not kick him out before his time.

11. The Apprentice

Sema slave. This is where I started, not even in the top ten. If you start here, just know you are the errands guy. You will be sent to River Road to buy 1/33 braids or no. 27 Angel braids, you will also run across the street to buy juice, coffee, smoothies, meat pies, chicken pies and snacks for clients. You will even babysit.

12. The Resident Hawker.

This is someone who has an agreement with the salon, the security guards and *Kanju* to provide extra services to the salon staff and clients. He is allowed to come and quietly whisper to a client. He might be selling pirated self-help books, gold-coated jewellery, doll shoes, second-hand panties, hot peanuts and peanut butter, or tights and leggings. This hawker mints money I tell you. They have studied the psychology of a woman at a salon and know that when women decide, "Today I'm going to the salon", it means they are going to treat themselves. While they are looking at themselves flirtingly as they get their hair done, they will want to keep the image by buying whatever comes their way. 'After all, you only live once, they will say as they hand you a thousand-shilling note to pay for their 800 bob worth of tops. And you, because you know how it works, pretend to look for change but don't get it, so you ask them to pick one more top for 200 bob. They happily do. It's just you and the hairdresser who know that, actually, these two tops she bought at 400 bob each, you can get for 30 bob, it's just that you have a good eye, you know your way around Gĩkomba and can iron a shirt as good as any French au pair that ever ironed a plaid skirt can.

Midlife crisis is very showy.
And it comes to you in different forms.
Inyitaga mūndū ta ngoma.

You start to wear dresses your teenage daughter wore when she was 10.

My aunt used to tell me,

'You, you have a nice body, you can wear anything.'

But me, me I love to be comfortable.

And you think you have time until you realise *unanusia* 43 *na haukai poa vile na hizi malinen.*

That's how you find all the 43 of yourself in a crop top walking along Muindi Mbingu Street.

And people look at your face, look at the crop top, look at the face again *halafu wanasema, 'Haithuru, inakaa* expensive, *si ya mtumba.'*

One of my younger friends told me she made a complete shift to string bikinis because

"This is the best I'll ever look in my life, so why waste it?"

I agree with her because there is no reason to show up like a shrivelled Pumba on either a public or private beach.

The other thing that becomes very difficult is the Queen's language.

Every time you speak English it exhausts you.
You wonder if you are really the same person who used to speak English like water.

And anytime you speak Kiswahili, it is a direct translation from your mother tongue.

That is the reason you hear people saying
"*Siyuko Leo.*"
Or "*Nipatilishie huto tufunguo.*"
Inī ūnengeririo tūcabi tūu.

Then you decide it is time to follow the American dream because, if not now then when?

Connections *tu ndio hauna.*
There is that one girl you went to primary school with and is your friend on Facebook, so you start to send her chats. You ask about the cost of living in Los Angeles. She says it's hard, and when she realizes that you may be following the American dream you start to get your blue ticks served early.

There is a message you archived three months ago and you go back to read it.

"Hi, I am an American Single father working for an NGO in Northern Kenya.

Looking for a Hardworking, Christian Kenyan lady over 35 years old.

To build a home with."

Ūkamenya direct, *Nīwe aracaria.*

A month later you are in Embu applying for a passport because the other one expired 14 years ago but *juu hakukuwa na pahali unaenda, imekuwa tu hapo kwa* drawers.
You buy goggles, *cia gwīkīraga* America *ūkīīrorera* snow.

Na tūnyatha twa jeans *twa gwīkīra hindī ya* Summer.

The American is actually a father of six. Two from his first marriage and four from his second (two sets of twins). *Mwatukanīra na ciaku igoka inya! Inyanya.*

You are now a mother of 8.

The first two are not children in the true sense of the word. They could, in fact, be considered your age mates.

You, you are not very worried about the age of the husband-to-be. *Akīrī mūthūngū. Mūthūngū kaī mūndū aroraga mīaka?*

Things actually work out, he even pays dowry to your uncles (as much dowry as any 45-year-old woman will be able to fetch) and you do one of those garden weddings *pale* Sigona Golf Club.

You in a white Cinderella gown, him in a Kitenge suit - *tūngī tūcoke gūtumwo nī a* Passion Fashions *na* Mutheu Apparels *tūhana* uniform *ya* Choir *ya* Seventh Day.

You even land in America but contrary to your expectations. Your expectations were that you knew you were going to New York City.

You find yourself in a village the equivalent of *Wīyūmīrīrie, kūndū kwīna kinya gīthīi.*

A posho meal, in America.
Your husband is a pig farmer, or raises pigs to supplement his pension and that posho mill will be your weekly excursion to mill food for the pigs.

O Monday, O Monday, *ūkaigīrīra kīondo gīa gathīka ng'ong'o Ūkauga haithuru,* at least it is overseas, nobody knows you here.

17. "Since My Cissterlocks Locked."

Since my Cissterlocks locked, people think I have money.
Even drivers when turning a tricky corner in the city will let me pass and then say, '*Ras, alafu?*'

Mimi I just laugh.

Even the *bangi* street guys in my county are not very frightening now, one of them will call out, '*Niaje empreeesss?*'

I will wave my hand and try to look agreeable.

And when I get into Cafe Kristina, the waiter pulls a chair for me. He probably supposes I am one of the Madams who bring in Turkey clothes in bulk. Or maybe I own a wholesale shop at Perida Center, and I've just landed from China with a shipment of skin whitening snail oil and snail creams and snail soaps to supply to the *small small* sellers in the front shops who call to you,

'*Madzam, mafuta.*'

When he brings me the menu, he probably thinks I'm going to order the 360 shillings Njahī stew.

Ndoī ndoka kuoha itha hau, waiting for my WhatsApp customers to respond to the photos I've posted.

Ingītisha kūrīa kīndū kīūmū ndainūka magūrū.

After walking up and down looking for a brooch worth as much as the Njahī, I needed to sit down. So when I order the *dawa,* I know he thinks I am probably on a tight dieting regimen with fancy ideas like intermittent fasting.

It's probably the reason I'm so trim, he thinks to himself and smiles at me when I slide some coins in the bill for his tip. Maybe I haven't converted my Shanghai money to Kenya shillings yet.

Angīmenya nī kwīnyerekia kūhīnjītie, ngīcaria mbia Nyairobi īno ndikahūndūke Kīeni kūrīmīra itūngūrū na mbura...

He would also pay me less attention if he saw *ile sufuria huwa nabandika gītheri nayo* twice a month.

Njoke ndīe njahī taūni, kaī ngūrūkaga?

I cook everything from scratch.

And I eat like a 65-year-old, health-conscious woman. Since my Cissterlocks locked, even Nyakati Sacco drivers speak carefully with me.

When me and my friends are standing there trying to decide which *matatu* to board,

They say,

'*Aria na Ras, ūcio nīwe ūkuuīte kībeti.* '
Ithuuri ciīho ndungu ciīna nda nene.

And when I am at the bus stop waiting for a *matatu* without a live disco to take me to town, the Metro Trans conductor, who has some dreadlocks tucked into a tight baseball hat (*ngūbia ya kīng'eti*), says to his *Kamagīra*

'*Tiga ihenya reke tūkuue kairītu.*'

And since it's not often I get called Kairītu, I feel very nice.

When you are closer to 40 than 20, the best you can get is *antiii* or *madamu īyo īrī na rasta.* If you are petit and trying to board 2NK then they will call you *nyina kana* to show deep respect because, of course, you have three 20-year-olds that are stressing you out *nīkīo ūnyihīte ūguo.*

Since my Cissterlocks locked, even the girls selling earrings and brooches call to me,

'Madam, *kuja tukuuzie.*'

They even allow me to take pictures of the brooches, thinking that I work in a bank *pale* Kenyatta Avenue and just coming to get these items to sell to my seniors at I&M Bank so I can get money for *chama*. If only they knew *nakuanga* hawker *huku wosap, hata hawangenisalimia.*

18. That Ka-aga Move Aside, Give Way For The Devil

And because *ndĩgũaga harĩa yaikio*,
You get to that place in your life where you now have a reliable,
loyal band of humans.

Not because you are a sweet pumpkin that spits rainbows,
but because you now know how to explain what you mean.

Now you have people who let you explain what you mean.

Now you are surrounded by people who tell you,

'*Aaai, ata kama ni kusave*, Cecilia, *mtu hukula kanyama*
sometimes.'

And you tell them,

'*Aaai* bro, *ata kama ni kuokoka*, bro, *mtu huwatch
kaseries* sometimes. *Ata kama ni* Leverage.'

You also learn to identify that *katone*. That *katone* that people who
make summaries of you without learning your backstory use, and
you learn to ignore it, or give straight comebacks.

That *katone* older women will take with 19-year-old girls when they think *hakuna kitu kwa kichwa,*

'*Wewe sasa ni msichana mkubwa, unafaa kuwa unafikiria* future *yako.*'

Even when they don't know that you work two jobs and go to night classes.

That *katone* an older woman will use on an unmarried woman of 31,

'*Wewe ujue unapitwa na maisha, unafaa kuwa umeolewa ukitunza mme.*'

You are now 40 and not bothered.

Because not everyone wants to know who you are.

And we don't have time to know what any one of us is really.

It takes time.

'*Patia Shetani njia apite*, then you go and treat yourself to a nice meal.' My friend says.

19. Plot 65 Stories: Story 1 When Death From A Teacher's Beating Was Chosen Over A Suspension

This is a true story.

n the village where I grew up, it was normal for people to call each other names.

Think of any wild animal.
Any ugly-looking animal.
It was fine.
Just don't call anyone a dog.
A dog was the mother of all insults.

If you were a student at Mitero Primary School, having a physical fight with someone and the word dog slipped out, the fight escalated to a whole new level. You stopped the physical fight and got into a word fight about your mothers and fathers and it got so ugly you had to call for support from boys from Kihuhīhīro Primary School, they were the *baddest*. They would come and beat up the side that had called the other "dog" and they would beat up everyone even remotely related to them.

So you could not say the word dog aloud.

A dog is called *Ngui*.

This dog in Kikuyu is *Ngui ĩno*.

These dogs are *Ngui ici*.

Thin rowdy dogs are *Magui maya*.

And now it had gotten out that we had said that a teacher had called the standard four students "dogs".

We had to define which dog.

'Did he say which one?' Our evening tuition teacher, my aunt asked.

'Yes, he called them thin mongrels.'

'So it was class four East?' My cousin asked.

'Yes, but he is also our Kiswahili teacher, so I'm sure he will call us too.' I proudly expressed.

I had just gotten to class four and had privileges. We now used ink pens and had music lessons. We ate school lunch, *Supro;* basic boiled *githeri*.

We also spoke in English.

By the first term, we had picked up the important phrases like:

'Please *teasher* can I go out.'

'Please give me a dot.'

A dot was a drop of ink your deskmate put for you when your pen ran out.

So I felt important, superior and better than my cousins who were still using pencils to write. Casper was speaking Kiswahili, him being in class three, but Melissa was still learning Kikuyu syllables in class one.

N *na* G *na* W *na* A - *Ngwa.*

Ala na E - Le.

Ngware.

Ngware is a Guinea pig.

That's how we learnt. You first learned Kikuyu as a language, and then the teacher used it to teach Kiswahili as a subject. Then you learnt Kiswahili as a language and it was used to teach English as a subject. Then in standard four, you started to learn English as a language.

So I proudly told my cousins the teacher had called the students dogs in English.

The most reserved teacher in the school had called students *Magui*.

So here were are, Casper and Me in the staffroom. He is screaming at one end of the staff room from the caning.

He is a class behind me so his class teacher is dealing with him. But I am in class four and I have to speak English and this case for the headteacher to deal with. The headmaster will write my name in the Black Book.

Meanwhile, one teacher is saying,

'Surely *Shishilia*, what will your grandmother say? You used to be a good girl, what happened? *Umemea pembe?*'

I want to tell her, '*Mwalimu tafadhali niue tu.*'
A death from a teacher would be better, I figured, and I would have told her as much if I wasn't completely tongue-tied.

I was angry at my cousin.

How could he have let this out?
I was thinking of the many ways to make his life miserable once we managed to get out of this without having my grandmother come to school.

That was the priority. *Cūcū* could not come to school, to any school.

I could just imagine appearing at the gate and finding *Cūcū* getting in the sheep's pen with a load of weeds as high as herself and me telling her, 'I did something wrong, you have to come to school.'
Anything but that.

'*Eh*, all the books that have been written you have finished! All that is remaining now is to talk about teachers. *Weeee, chunga sana.*'

She would say.

Then she would start a prologue,

'You children, play with education. Play with education completely. Me, my father did not take me to school because I was a girl. That is why I have to scratch this ground from morning till evening with this *panga*. You, you want to play. Do you have a *shamba*? Me, my husband got me this *shamba*. You, where will you go if you don't read? *Eh*? Me if I had read, I would have done better, so it is your loss if you don't want to read. Me, my work I have done. Have you ever slept hungry?'

'No.'

The lecture went straight to the brain and made you feel more pain than if she actually took a rod and canned you.

Now I was in the staffroom being caned. This hand, then that hand, then some more scolding from other teachers.

Casper is pleading for his life.

'*Mwalimu* please *usinichape, sitarudia kusema uongo.*'

We had lied, we said.

The teacher we had spread the rumour about now took us out of the staffroom for proper questioning.

'*Shishilia*, did you hear me call anyone Mongrels?'

'No teacher, someone said you did.'

'Who is this and what class are they in?'

'*Mwalimu,* this person is not even in this school, so I am sure it's a lie.'

I was not going to say where I had heard it from.

The upper classes had a mobile library. I had managed to wriggle my way in to borrow storybooks at lunchtime. So, I heard things.

I shot my cousin a glance again to tell him, "Dare you say this is not true!"

'My aunt from Marmernet told me.'

Said I.

'What is the name of this aunt?' The teacher quizzed.

'Leah.' I said.

'She was a student here, many years ago,' I continued, 'and when she came to visit us, and I said the name of our Kiswahili teacher, she said that.'

'When will this aunt come again?'

'Maybe at Christmas, *Mwalimu,* but she was pregnant so she might not come this time.'

I am sure he read through the weak storyline but I had given it my all.

'You will have to go and call your *cūcū* to come.'

'*Woooi Mwalimu,* please, we are sorry. Beat us. Then punish us.

Please please please, don't ask us to call *cūcū*.'

We got off, I thought we got off easily and we didn't talk about it until two days later. On coming home I heard *Cūcū* telling her friend,

'Shiriba, these are not children. These are trials. What shall I do? I will die completely.'

And *Cūcū* Shiriba was saying,

'Ah, children? Children are like that. They lie sometimes but they don't mean harm.'

'No, no *aiiiii*, they will make demons come out of me!' *Ngūkiumūo ni ngoma biū.*

I knew that suddenly peace had vanished from our home. We were finished!

Cūcū is smart and she can play with your mind *hadi* you tell her things you didn't intend for her to know but, because she is acting like she knows everything, you just confess.

So for two days, she didn't say anything, until Friday night when she was putting us to bed.

I was the eldest so when the two slept, a flood of pinches fell upon me.

'You hypocrite of a child. You think I don't know! You think I don't know anything! You have embarrassed me in this entire country. '*Ūkanjonorothia būrūri mūgima*! What kind of a child are you? Do you have a good head? *Eh*? I'm asking you? What is this I've heard?'

So the story came out.

I couldn't try the story about Aunt Leah on her. So I told her the truth.

I had heard it from a boy. The boy was in standard seven. This was his name.

'*Eh*? What business do you have being with boys! Let me ever catch you listening to boys. *Ihīī*? Look at her!'

A few more pinches. A few more dirty looks. Then she added, 'From today, I never want you to listen to boys' stories. And women's stories too. Mind your own business.'

Many times *Cūcū* would be in the middle of a story with some woman, and I would be sat there for an hour, two hours, or three hours and I was not supposed to listen.

I learnt to daydream. I guess that is the reason why I end up zoning out when I am with people. I could be sitting in a group of people and I have no clue what they are talking about. I prefer it though. I can swing in and out of small talk without commitment.

Casper got his beating the following day. He was given a different law, to keep things spoken within Plot 65 in.
How the story got out was, being the newsmaker he was, he decided to find out whether the teacher called students other insults apart from dogs. And who better to ask than the teacher's daughter. Lol.

We had suddenly become the scum of the earth, but it only lasted a short while before we did something else of consequence than the one before.

Cūcū Shiriba suggested that my *cūcū* join her church so that she could attend Wednesday prayer meetings, where they prayed *na Kīīroho* and even cast out demons.

Plot 65 Tales, Story 2: Animal Farm

My mother has a favourite saying.
She will be in the middle of an engaging story and she will say,

'You should have seen her! She jumped five feet up and denied everything!'

Or she will be saying how something would never work out if you involved a particular person. '*Ai*, That one! That one will jump you like pole vaulting! He/she cannot be trusted.'

She swears a lot too. I thought her dog's name was *Niga* when I was small.

She would be like, '*Nigaa*! *Gerrout wewe*!'

She also called my grandmother's sheep '*Maniga maya*.' But really, I didn't take it as an insult, I don't know, I guess I thought it's like when you cannot remember something's name and call it something similar. So what did I think was a *Niga*?

Ok. I don't.

This was not about niggas.

I was thinking about the expression, how after you have agreed on something with someone they turn around and say, 'Who? Me? *Aii hapana.*' And they leave you standing there doubting your memory.

Then I was wondering where she gets such expressions, but I remembered.
She was an athlete. Mostly practising over the fences on their farm. But she might also have come up with them during the nine months she spent waiting for me to be born after my father had jumped five feet up and asked, 'Who? Me?' And said *Sayonara*.

But we are elastic. Me, my mother and her mother before that. We get on that pole and propel ourselves forward, no matter the odds.

Yes, we break our backs,
And legs,
And arms,
And toes,
And heart,
But not our will!

So when my bro saw the nigga story he said I should mention that, in spite of the expletives, the adults in our family are religious. And it can be proven by how quickly our grandmother calls out to Maria whenever she is in danger.

She will be chewing her dry sweet potatoes, without tea and chokes on her own saliva.

'Maria!' She calls out.

'What is it?' Someone will ask.

'Ah, is it not this small sweet potato that wants to kill me!'

'But *Cūcū, si* I said there is tea but you said you don't want?'

'Ah, cold tea? I don't want heartburn.' She will explain and choke again. And dare you laugh, or not say *pole*.

'*Ng'undeno*! You are just sitting there watching me die and you can't even warm some tea for me? *Mbūri*!'

Ng'unda is a donkey.

Mbūri is a goat.

So you quickly run behind the house to get some tiny pieces of sticks to kindle the fire and warm her tea.

You come and warm her some tea but by that time she has finished the sweet potatoes.

So you venture to say, '*Cūcū*, let me just drink the tea.'

'*Ngūrwe! Nongīmuona*! When I drink tea, it is the same as if I spill on the floor, eh? You thankless child *phu*!'

So you pour her the tea and walk away feeling like the ass she has called you.

Ngúrūwe is a wild pig.

And rightly so. I have often felt like a wild pig. Black, Misplaced and Nocturnal.

Then we all sit around the fire waiting for the *mūkimo* to boil as we listen to *matangazo ya vifo* (obituaries) on Kameme FM.

We are a family that has always been surrounded by animals, strays find their way into our home, both animal and human strays, I should say.

But it is the personalities of these animals that have always amazed me. When you have a pet, it is very likely they will take up on your personality. Like, I have always had cats that really respect my space. They walk around the house stealthily without making noise unless I am also making noise.

Our animals at home were not any different. The only thing was that they were not just cats and dogs, but sheep and chickens and turkeys and cows too.

One of the most amusing sheep we have is called Nyamūthere. Nyamūthere is the great great great grand-daughter of the original Nyamūthere who was a sheep that stood as high as halfway up the kitchen door, and only needed to use her head to lift the door clutch. She would get into the kitchen, turn over the *sufuria* of hot *gītheri*, and wait for it to cool down, then she would eat every grain, then drink the soup at the bottom. Then she would tilt the tea kettle open and drink the tea. That, in a span of less than 20 minutes. If you had gone to the *shamba* to pick up a cabbage so that you could come and fry the *gītheri* for the people working hard on the farm, you would now have to look for a recipe with just two ingredients, cabbage and potatoes. *Na ndūrī ūndū ūngīamīkire, tondū akīrī we ūtigire riko ūgūo.* Now we have one of Nyamūthere's grandsons, a free spirit who has a way of escaping from the rest of the herd to eat plums.

He is never around. You find him eating tomatoes or lucerne in the middle of the farm.

But the cup went to our dog, Tom. (Most of our dogs are Tom and Shimba) There was Tom who played the psycho *hadi tukainua mikono*. Tom would find a way to get into the kitchen and get a whole container of Blue Band, carry it to his shed and sit there eating it as if he bought it with his own money. He would set up the younger dog, Shimba, and we were none the wiser. When the rabbits gave birth, Tom, who knew how to slide open the door, would open the door, and the younger dog would think "Hurray! Manna from Heaven!" and chomp down the tiny things while Tom watched from his hatch. Shimba would of course be caught and given a beating.

One time, someone left a Thermos flask in the tree farm, Tom carefully brought the thermos, with *tumandazi* in a bag and laid them at the washing station.

We were so confused for many days. My aunt was sure *kuna mtu anajaribu kuturoga* because how do you explain a dog carrying a hot thermos of tea?

The owner of the thermos was eventually found and, of course when Aunt tried to explain the story, people became convinced that *aya makoragwo marī arogi ona wamona hau.*

Then we had a turkey that got high from giving someone a kick from the back. You would be walking ahead carrying a *sufuria* full of dirty utensils then you would fall *"koto!"* and drop the *sufuria* while the turkey trumpeted away happily. You would actually hear him laugh happily.

There was a cat that loved music. She was called Goo Goo Doll, but I called her Kajuju. When she was pregnant, she learned how to turn on the CD player. The CD player had a Westlife CD in it, and if you were in the kitchen, you would hear, "An empty street, an empty sky, a hole inside my head…" *Kumbe*… I told my mother that Kajuju knew how to turn on the CD player and she snorted. Until one Saturday, while she was watching politics on TV, Kajuju came and rubbed her hip on the play button, then climbed on top of the radio to listen to her Boy Band in peace. My mother called me, whispering,

'*Ngai,* Gathoni. *Nyau nīyahingūrīra redio!'*

'*Ini īī ndiakwirire nīyūūī.'*

'*Nūū wamīonirie?'*

'*Īkīrī njūgī.'*

She had never had such a fright in her life.

But that's the thing with animals, we just assume they are simply governed by instinct and have no real abilities. I believe differently, I guess in that regard I am a white person, and I can't wait for the time when I will have enough time to study animal behaviour. Especially the cat family.

20. Day Drinking With My Neighbours

I won't admit that I was day drinking with neighbours and friends, *tuseme tu*, I had a typical middle-class Kenyan weekend where we sat and mixed whiskey and Sprite and said -if only we had a car-

'If only we had a car, we would not be here.'
'Walai hatungekuwa hapa.'
'We would be parked at Kamakis ordering ribs.'
'Or even in Rongai eating pork.'
'Sio kukunywa masoda hapa kwa plot.'